国务院侨务办公室立项
彭磷基外招生人才培养改革基金资助

外贸函电

Business Correspondence

陈岩峰　Shirin Boroumand Selph　编著

暨南大學出版社
JINAN UNIVERSITY PRESS

中国·广州

图书在版编目（CIP）数据

外贸函电/陈岩峰，Shirin Boroumand Selph 编著．—广州：暨南大学出版社，2013.9

ISBN 978－7－5668－0513－3

Ⅰ．①外…　Ⅱ．①陈…②S．…　Ⅲ．①对外贸易—英语—电报信函—写作　Ⅳ．①H315

中国版本图书馆 CIP 数据核字（2013）第 044496 号

出版发行：暨南大学出版社

地　址：中国广州暨南大学
电　话：总编室（8620）85221601
营销部（8620）85225284　85228291　85228292（邮购）
传　真：（8620）85221583（办公室）　85223774（营销部）
邮　编：510630
网　址：http://www.jnupress.com　http://press.jnu.edu.cn

排　版：广州市天河星辰文化发展部照排中心
印　刷：佛山市浩文彩色印刷有限公司

开　本：787mm×960mm　1/16
印　张：8.75
字　数：160 千
版　次：2013 年 9 月第 1 版
印　次：2013 年 9 月第 1 次
印　数：1—2000 册

定　价：20.00 元

CONTENTS

Unit 1 Rules of a Good Writing ······ 1
1.1 Introduction ······ 1
1.2 Principles of writing a business letter ······ 1
1.3 The writing process ······ 4

Unit 2 Structure of a Business Letter ······ 12
2.1 Introduction ······ 12
2.2 The main parts ······ 12
2.3 Miscellaneous matters ······ 18

Unit 3 Addressing the Envelope ······ 22
3.1 Introduction ······ 22
3.2 The envelope ······ 22
3.3 The recipient's address ······ 23
3.4 The return address ······ 23
3.5 Other inclusions ······ 23

Unit 4 Forms of Business Letter ······ 25
4.1 Introduction ······ 25
4.2 The block form ······ 25
4.3 The indented form ······ 26
4.4 The semi-block form ······ 27
4.5 The simplified form ······ 28

Unit 5 Establishing Business Relations ······ 30
5.1 Introduction ······ 30
5.2 Information channel ······ 30

5.3 Types of letters …… 31
5.4 Letter content …… 31
5.5 Sample letters …… 32
5.6 Word study …… 33
5.7 Useful sentences …… 34

Unit 6 Inquiries and Replies …… 36
6.1 Introduction …… 36
6.2 Types of inquiry …… 36
6.3 Responses to inquiries …… 36
6.4 Notes …… 38
6.5 Sample letters …… 39
6.6 Word study …… 40
6.7 Useful sentences …… 42

Unit 7 Quotations …… 44
7.1 Introduction …… 44
7.2 Letter content …… 44
7.3 Notes …… 45
7.4 Sample letters …… 45
7.5 Word study …… 48
7.6 Useful sentences …… 49

Unit 8 Sales Letters …… 51
8.1 Introduction …… 51
8.2 Types of sales letters …… 51
8.3 Notes …… 52
8.4 Sample letters …… 54
8.5 Word study …… 56
8.6 Useful sentences …… 57

Unit 9 Offers …… 59
9.1 Introduction …… 59
9.2 Types of offers …… 59

9.3 Letter content …… 59
9.4 Sample letters …… 61
9.5 Word study …… 62
9.6 Useful sentences …… 64

Unit 10 Counter Offers …… 66
10.1 Introduction …… 66
10.2 Letter content …… 66
10.3 Notes …… 67
10.4 Sample letters …… 67
10.5 Word study …… 68
10.6 Useful sentences …… 69

Unit 11 Orders …… 71
11.1 Introduction …… 71
11.2 Letter content …… 71
11.3 Dealing with the first order …… 72
11.4 Notes …… 72
11.5 Sample letters …… 73
11.6 Word study …… 75
11.7 Useful sentences …… 76

Unit 12 Complaints …… 79
12.1 Introduction …… 79
12.2 Types of complaints …… 79
12.3 Letter content …… 80
12.4 Notes …… 80
12.5 Dealing with a complaint …… 80
12.6 Sample letters …… 81
12.7 Word study …… 82
12.8 Useful sentences …… 83

Unit 13 Claims …… 85
13.1 Introduction …… 85

13. 2 Rules for filing a claim ······ 85
13. 3 Dealing with a claim ······ 86
13. 4 Sample letters ······ 86
13. 5 Word study ······ 89
13. 6 Useful sentences ······ 91

Unit 14 Insurance ······ 94
14. 1 Introduction ······ 94
14. 2 Notes ······ 94
14. 3 Sample letters ······ 95
14. 4 Word study ······ 97
14. 5 Useful sentences ······ 98

Unit 15 Shipment ······ 100
15. 1 Introduction ······ 100
15. 2 Letter content ······ 100
15. 3 Types of letters ······ 101
15. 4 Notes ······ 102
15. 5 Sample letters ······ 103
15. 6 Word study ······ 104
15. 7 Useful sentences ······ 106

Unit 16 Container Service ······ 108
16. 1 Introduction ······ 108
16. 2 Advantages of container service ······ 108
16. 3 Packing ······ 109
16. 4 Marking ······ 110
16. 5 Sample letters ······ 111
16. 6 Word study ······ 112
16. 7 Useful sentences ······ 113

Unit 17 Payment ······ 115
17. 1 Introduction ······ 115
17. 2 The procedures for issuing L/C ······ 115

17. 3 The content of a L/C 116
17. 4 Urging the establishment of L/C 117
17. 5 L/C amendments and extensions 117
17. 6 Sample letters 118
17. 7 Word study 120
17. 8 Useful sentences 122

Unit 18 Sales Contract 124
18. 1 Introduction 124
18. 2 Content of the contract 124
18. 3 Types of contracts 125
18. 4 Sample letters 125
18. 5 Word study 127
18. 6 Useful sentences 128

References 130

Unit 1　Rules of a Good Writing

1.1　Introduction

Writing effective business letters is an essential skill for all business people who engage in the international trade. It defines and solidifies all aspects of the business partnership, including trade negotiations, the conditions and expectations between exporters and importers. Although the current popularity of communication via the Internet, telephone and fax is widely used in the international economic exchange and trade activities, the international business letters are still of particular importance.

The four main functions of a business letter are:

1) to convey or to ask for information;

2) to make or to accept an offer;

3) to deal with details concerning business negotiations;

4) to remind the recipient of the sender's existence.

Therefore, a well-written business letter is an essential tool for companies engaged in the foreign trade and commercial activities. Students majoring in International Trade and Business English should learn the basic principles and procedures of writing a business letter.

1.2　Principles of writing a Business letter

The principles for writing an effective business letter include clarity, conciseness, courtesy, completeness, and accuracy.

1.2.1　Clarity

The primary goal of a business letter is to state your purpose clearly, so that the letter is not misunderstood. When you are sure about what you want to say, express yourself in plain, straightforward, and simple words. When the writer expresses himself or herself more clearly, the reader understands more easily and can respond more quickly. Thus, the process of communication becomes more efficient. **To achieve clarity, the writer needs to pay close attention to the following guidelines:**

1) Make sure that the sentence is structured properly to convey what you want to communicate;
2) Do not use ambiguous sentences and needless jargon; instead, try to use plain, simple words and short sentences;
3) Each paragraph should contain only one idea and should flow naturally into the next paragraph.

If you can follow the above guidelines, you will have clarity in your business letter writing.

1.2.2 Conciseness

Conciseness means writing or saying something in the fewest words. To achieve this, try to avoid wordiness or redundancy. Clarity and conciseness often go hand-in-hand. The elimination of wordy business jargon can make a letter easier to read and help eliminate misunderstandings. The author should use straightforward words to replace complex phrases or clauses. Wherever possible, choose the single word over the elaborate phrase. Your goal should be to express yourself in simple language so that your message is clear at first reading. The purpose of writing a letter is to make yourself understood easily, not to show how you can write long and complicated sentences. However, a concise letter is not necessarily a short one. Sometimes a letter dealing with a multiplicity of matters cannot avoid being long.

1.2.3 Courtesy

Courtesy means being polite; of course, it is important in business correspondence writing. Being polite is a basic principle of business. The courteous writer should be sincere and tactful, thoughtful and appreciative. Courtesy is not only using polite phrases such as "your kind inquiry", "your esteemed order", or "your valued customer", but also showing consideration for your correspondent. Courtesy is the quality that enables us to decline to do a favor and at the same time keep a friend or to refuse a customer's request for credit without sacrificing all hope of future business.

Reply to all correspondence promptly. If possible, answer them the same day you receive them. It is impolite to keep your correspondent waiting for an answer. If you cannot deal promptly with a letter seeking information, explain why and when you will write again. This creates an impression of efficiency and helps to build a goodwill.

Try to understand and respect your correspondent's point of view; resist the temptation to insist that you are right and they are wrong. If his or her suggestions are unfounded or their criticisms seem unfair, carefully construct your reply with tasteful restraint and convey your point of view without sounding offensive. If you receive correspondence that is rude or sharply worded, resist the temptation to reply in similar terms. Instead, answer the letter courteously; you lower your dignity if you allow the writer to set the tone of your reply.

Two people or parties, who are doing business together, have both common and contradictory interests. It is very important to keep in mind distinctions between overlapping concepts: courtesy overdone may amount to flattery and sincerity overdone may amount to featherbrain. In short, any virtue overdone will produce some undesirable effect, and propriety is the watchword in distinguishing the right course from the wrong.

1.2.4 Completeness

A business letter is successful and functions well only when it contains all the necessary information. An outline helps you write a full and complete letter. Thoroughly review the letter to ensure that it contains all the details that have been discussed, and answer all of your client's questions. Incompleteness is impolite, and can create an unfavorable impression of your company. The client may decide to work with a different firm that can provide them with all of the information needed to make educated business decisions.

To achieve completeness, keep the following questions in mind: Why are you writing the letter? Have you answered your client's questions clearly and precisely? Did you include facts supporting your statements? Did you communicate clearly what you expect from the reader? Use specific facts and figures, choose vivid, image-building words, and make sure you use modifiers in the right place. If you have given the answers to all these questions, you have a complete letter.

1.2.5 Accuracy

A business letter must contain appropriate and grammatically correct sentences as well as factual and accurate information. While you are proofreading the document, special attention should be paid to form and convention, as well as to content. Double check the spelling of articles, specifications, quantities, and anything else that specifically apply to the message you are conveying. To avoid common grammatical errors in business writing, pay special attention to how you use pronouns, adjectives, articles, verbs, adverbs, conjunctions, and participles.

Factual errors are the result of lack of careful attention. Errors in price quotations or delivery dates are oversights caused by careless typing and insufficient proofreading. To avoid mistakes, use a variety of references to check and recheck your facts.

Careful attention to details, thorough proofreading, and the diligent use of references will eliminate errors in business letter writing.

1.3 The writing process

1.3.1 Preparation

1) What are your reader's interests

When writing a business letter, it is very important to know your reader's interests. Ask yourself, what is the reader's cultural and economic background? When you have found out your reader's interests, think about how you can adapt your message to one that your reader will understand from his or her perspective. To adapt your message, begin by visualizing your reader. Form a mental picture of what the reader knows about the subject, what his or her educational level is, and how he or she thinks. Your correspondence must create a good first impression. To achieve this, "put yourself in the reader's shoes" and try to imagine how he will react to what you write. Constantly ask yourself, "What are the reader's needs, wishes, interests, problems, and how can I successfully meet them" and "If I were to receive this letter, how would I feel about it".

The following paragraphs are **examples** from the annual reports of two different companies. The writer of the first report apparently viewed his readers as not being well-informed in finance. The writer of the second report regarded his readers as being well-informed in finance, such as stockbrokers, financial managers, financial analysts, and bankers.

Paragraph ①

The company had a total sale of 117 million dollars in 2009, which was slightly higher than 2008. After deducting all expenses, the company had a net balance of 380, 458 dollars. The increase in profits allowed the company to increase your annual dividend payments 50 cents per share paid over the last 10 years.

Paragraph ②

The total of investments and advances in three unconsolidated corporate subsidiaries and the 50% owned companies was 42 million dollars as of December 31, 2009. The excess investments in certain companies over the net asset value were $189, 000. The corporation's equity in the net assets as of December 31, 2010 was 49 million dollars.

What do you think about the writing? Which one is clearer? Perhaps you think each one is good, perhaps you do not understand both of them. The answer depends upon who read them. Use different words for different audiences, and that is what you should try to do.

2) Collect related information

Collect the information that you may need to refer to when writing your letter, such as past correspondence, information from other employees that have knowledge of the company you are writing to, sales and inventory records, warranties, and product descriptions. Then, use the collected information to evaluate an applicant, acknowledge an offer and predict the reader's reaction. After referring to the information you gathered, try to impartially judge what the reader's reaction will be: positive, negative or somewhere in between. You can't be sure of what the reader's response will be to your letter's objective. The only thing you can do is apply your knowledge of the reader to a specific situation and use your best judgment.

3) Plan your letter

Many business letters are short and routine and can be written or dictated without any special preparation, while others must first be thought about and planned. Jot down all the points you wish to cover and then arrange them in a logical order so that your letter can be read smoothly and fluently. If your letter is in reply to one received, underline those parts which seek information, or on which comments are necessary. This will ensure that your reply is complete and easy to understand.

1.3.2 Writing effectively

As we have already mentioned, it is important to keep in mind the principles for effective business letter writing. Let us go into further details on how to apply these principles to write more effectively.

1) Choose the right tone

Tone is the manner of expression in speech or writing. If a letter is to achieve its purpose, its tone must be right. Before writing, think carefully about the way you want to influence your reader. You should use right tone and adopt proper attitude. Ask yourself, what do you want this letter to do, and then express yourself accordingly. Being persuasive, apologetic, obliging, firm and so on, depending on the effect you want to produce.

2) Write naturally and sincerely

When you write or dictate a business letter, try to create a genuine interest in the person you are writing to, concerning his or her problems and challenges. Be sincere; say what you have to say with sincerity and respect. Express your thoughts in your own words and in your own way. Be yourself. In this way what you say would sound natural if read over the telephone.

3) Prefer the active voice to the passive one

Generally speaking, an active voice is preferred rather than a passive voice. An active voice conveys stronger and livelier ideas. Using the active voice, the subject does the action while in passive voice it receives the action. **For example**:

(1) The results were reported in our July 9th letter.
(2) We reported the results in our July 9th letter.
(3) Our office would like this problem to be brought before the board.
(4) This office requests that the secretary bring this problem before the board.

However, your decision on which kind of tone to be used is not simply a matter of choice.

4) Use effective words

Wordiness is expressing a statement in more words than necessary. Make it a rule to use no more words than needed to make your meaning clear. Today's business people receive many letters and welcome a letter that is direct and to the point. First, think about what you want to say and then state it naturally without frills. Write your business correspondence in a way that the reader will understand what you are trying to say clearly as if you were in conversation with him or her. Keep your sentences short and avoid the frequent use of such conjunctions as "and", "but", "however" and "consequently".

Compare the following pairs of sentences:

(1) Please be good enough to advise me. (Wordy)

(2) Please advise me. (Concise)

(3) We are eagerly awaiting the favor of your early reply. (Wordy)

(4) We await your reply. (Concise)

(5) We are in receipt of the letter you sent to us dated June 2020. (Wordy)

(6) We received your letter of June 20. (Concise)

Familiar words are everyday words that have sharp and clear meanings. Use words that most people use in everyday conversation. In order to create effective communication, avoid stiff and difficult words that do not communicate well. However, at times, difficult words are not all bad. They should be used when they can define your needs accurately and precisely. **The following contrasting examples** illustrate the communication advantages of familiar words over less familiar ones.

(1) This machine has a tendency to develop excessive and unpleasant audible symptoms when operating at elevated temperatures. (Unfamiliar)

(2) This machine tends to get noisy when it runs hot. (Familiar)

(3) The most operative assembly line configuration is a unidirectional flow. (Unfamiliar)

(4) The most efficient assembly line design is a one-way flow. (Familiar)

(5) The conclusion ascertained from a perusal of pertinent data is that a lucrative market exists for the product. (Unfamiliar)

(6) The data studied shows that the product is in good demand. (Familiar)
(7) Company operations for the preceding accounting period terminated with a substantial deficit. (Unfamiliar)
(8) The company lost a good deal of money last year. (Familiar)

5) Avoid commercial jargon

Avoid using statements and vague phrases that add little or nothing to the reason behind your correspondence. Such phrases were at one time common, but they have no place in the modern business letter. You can see some examples in the unfamiliar phrases in the preceding section.

6) Write with consistency and clarity

Be consistent in writing business letters. Avoid repeating words in the same sentence or paragraph. However, in your effort to avoid repeating, do not make the opposite mistake of confusing your reader by using different words to express exactly the same thing. Do not state in the same letter that goods have been sent, forwarded, and dispatched. If you begin your letter by referring to a company, Do not change it as you go along into a "firm" or a "business" or an "organization". If you do, you will leave your reader wondering whether something different is intended.

Preciseness is also required in a business letter. Use expressions with precise meanings. When acknowledging a letter, refer to it by date, subject, and reference number (if any). When referring to a date, mention the month by name and avoid using a numeric alternative. For example, use "October 25, 2009" instead of "10/25/2009".

Compare the following sentences:

(1) As to the steamers sailing from Hong Kong to Sydney, we have bimonthly direct service. (Ambiguous)
(2) We have two direct sailings every month from Hong Kong to Sydney. (Clear)

7) Avoid monotony

Monotony means uniformity or lack of variation in pitch, intonation, or inflection. In a business letter, you should use sentences that will make your message vivid. Short sentences are preferable to long ones, because short sentences are easily understood. A succession of short sentences, however, has an unpleasant jerky effect. The best letters are those that provide a mixture of sentences in different lengths. If you wish to emphasize specific words, place them at the beginning of a sentence. **For example**, "I met your director yesterday" is the common sentence structure. Changing the word order in the sentence into "Yesterday I met your director" emphasizes the specific time (yesterday).

Emphasis is also achieved by using "it is" or "it was" to introduce statements. **For instance**, "The goods did not arrive on time, unfortunately" is the common sentence structure. "It was unfortunate that the goods did not arrive in time," emphasizes "unfortunate" which tells the reader your feelings.

8) Limit sentence content

Limiting sentence content is largely a matter of mentally selecting thoughts and ideas in a sentence and then deciding which should go into separate sentences. However, you can combine thoughts into one sentence only when your thoughts are closely related or when you de-emphasize the content. **For instance**:

(1) This memorandum is being distributed with the first semester class cards, which are to serve as a final check on the correct registration of students and are to be used later as the mid-semester grade cards, which are to be submitted prior to November 17. (Long and hard to understand)

(2) This memorandum is being distributed with the first-semester class cards. These cards will now serve as the final check on student registration. Later, they will be used for mid-semester grades, which are due before November 17. (Short and clear)

9) Use a topic sentence

An effective way of organizing paragraphs is to use a topic sentence, which expresses the main idea of the paragraph. The remaining sentences have the function of developing the topic. Using a topic sentence forces you to find the central idea of each paragraph.

A topic sentence usually appears at the beginning of each paragraph. It can also appear at the end of a sentence. By studying the subject of your sentences, you can determine whether the topic sentence should be presented first or at the conclusion of the statement.

10）Avoid unrelated ideas in one sentence

If two unrelated ideas are expressed in one sentence, it will create confusion.

To have harmony, unrelated ideas should not be presented together; each idea should be expressed by one clear thought in separate sentences. You can relate the two ideas in your sentence by putting the ideas in separate sentences; making one of the ideas subordinate to the other and adding words that show how the ideas are related. **For example**:

Mr. Wang is our sales manager and he has a degree in law.

Perhaps the two ideas are related, but we can't see the relationship from the words. **A better arrangement is to put each idea in a separate sentence**:

Mr. Wang is our sales manager. He has a law degree.

Sometimes the two ideas can be kept in one sentence by subordinating one to the other. **For example**:

Mr. Wang, our sales manager, has a law degree.

11）Pay attention to first and last impressions

If you are writing a letter in reply to another, acknowledge in your opening paragraph that you have received the letter by commenting on one of that letter's primary statements or ideas. Avoid the old-fashioned phrases, **such as** "we are in receipt of your letter ..." or "we acknowledge your letter ...". Although they are grammatically correct, they tend to be dull and monotonous. If a letter has been well planned and follows a logical sequence, a brief observation (such as a comment or remark) will usually be enough to provide an effective ending. A word of caution! Avoid the kind of ending introduced by a participle. "Thanking you in advance" and similar endings are no longer used in modern letter-writing. They serve no useful purpose.

1.3.3 Review your letters

Be careful to create a good first impression in each letter you write. Before signing the letter, check it for content accuracy and test its general suitability by asking yourself the following questions.

1) Is its appearance attractive?

2) Is it well laid out?

3) Is the spelling and punctuation correct?

4) Does it cover all essential points and is the information given correct?

5) Is it clear, concise and courteous?

6) Does it sound natural and sincere?

7) Does it adopt the reader's point of view and will it be readily understood?

8) Does the general tone create the impression intended?

9) Would I like this letter if I were in the reader's place?

If the answers to all these questions are "yes", then the letter will be the first step in creating goodwill; you can safely sign and send it.

Unit 2 Structure of a Business Letter

2.1 Introduction

The structure of an international business letter still follows a pattern that is determined by certain rules. However, in modern times, the style has become friendlier and more personal. The choice of layout is a matter of individual taste, but it is better to follow established formats that the business world is accustomed to. **A well-arranged business letter usually consists of seven basic parts**:

1) The letterhead;
2) The date;
3) The inside name and address;
4) The salutation;
5) The message;
6) The complimentary close;
7) The writer's signature and his official company position.

Besides these parts, sometimes a business letter may include some other elements, such as reference number, for the attention of, subject heading, enclosure, identification mark, postscript, margins, the second page style, etc.

2.2 The main parts

2.2.1 The Letterhead

The letterhead you use expresses your firm's characteristics. It helps the reader to form his or her impression of your company. Styles are different in some way, but they all give similar information, including the name and address of the firm, and some related information like telephone number, fax number, email address, and website address. The company trademark or slogan is typically on letterhead and helps define your business.

Business organizations select their letterhead style carefully. They aim for a certain effect that defines its corporate identity and fits the image the company is attempting to project. Specially designed letterhead can contribute a great deal to a business letter's initial impact on the receiver. It can set a tone for what follows. It is then up to the writer to maintain that good impression. **For example:**

China National Textiles Import & Export Corporation
Zhuhai branch
128 Jinghui Road, Xiangzhou
Zhuhai City 519002
Guangdong Province
China
E-mail address: little-fox-textiles. Love@ 163. com
Cable address: TEXTILE GDZHUHAI

2. 2. 2 The date

You can write a date in English in two styles. The standard order of typing the date in the United States is month, day, and year. Between the day and the year, use a comma. **For example:**

(1) September 9, 2009.
(2) January 24, 2012.
(3) April 21, 2010.

In Britain, the standard order is day, month, and year. **For example:**

(1) 12 September, 2010.
(2) 12th September, 2010.

For the day, either cardinal numbers (1, 2, 3, 4, etc.) or ordinal numbers (1st, 2nd, 3rd, 4th, etc.) have been used. **For example:**

(1) March 1st, 2011 or March 1, 2011.

(2) April 3rd, 2011 or April 3, 2011.

The month and year should not be written in their abbreviated form or it could cause confusion. To give the date in figures only is not professional. **For example**, "12/9/2010". In the United States, it may mean December 9, 2010, but in European countries, it means September 12, 2010. Therefore, if you use numbers to express the date, it is very easy to cause confusion.

2.2.3 The inside name and address

The inside name and address should include some or all parts of the following: the name of the recipient, company's name, suite or room number, street address, city, country, and postal code. Using correct postal codes helps facilitate mechanical mail sorting. The inside name and address appears on the left margin and usually starts one or two lines below the date.

Precede the addressee's name with a courtesy title, **such as** "Mr.", "Ms.", or "Dr.". When you do not know the identity of that person, omit the courtesy title and give the full name. If you do not know the appropriate head of department, address the letter to him by his official title, **For example**:

Sales Manager
The Red Flag Engineering CO. Ltd.
208 Qianshan Road, Xiangzhou District
Zhuhai City 519001
Guangdong,
China

When you address a letter to a person, be certain the spelling of his name is correct.

English addresses may have some or all of **the following parts**:

1) House name;

2) House number;

3) Street number;

4) Name of city or town;

5) Name of state and its postal code;

6) Name of country.

When writing to a foreign country, make sure you always include the name of the country. Even if the city mentioned is very famous, or is the country's capital. **For example**:

The Sales Manager
The Red Flag Company Limited
24 South Bank
Birmingham
Alabama
U. S. A.

Here "Birmingham" may refer to at least three cities; you should make clear about this. First, Birmingham Can refer to a city in central England. It is a major industrial center and transportation hub. Second, Birmingham may be a city in Alabama in the USA. This is the largest city in the state of Alabama; it is in a mining and industrial region. Third, Birmingham may also be a city in southeast Michigan in the USA, a residential suburb of Detroit.

There are specific rules for the use of titles. "Esq." (for Esquire) is reserved for a particular profession such as attorneys, lawyers, judges, magistrates, or barristers. "Mr." or "Ms." should be used before a name, **for example**, "Mr. John Carlson". "Esq." should follow a name. Between "Esq." and the name, there is a comma. As in "John Carlson, Esq.", the latter form is considered more polite in England, but most Americans do not use it.

If you address a man, we suggest you use the courtesy title "Mr.". If you write to a married woman, use "Mrs.", and an unmarried woman, use "Miss". However, nowadays, most women, especially professional women, prefer "Ms.".

2.2.4 The salutation

The salutation is a greeting word or phrase to start a letter. It is usually positioned on the left side of the sheet, about a double space below the inside address.

Although a business letter tends to be friendlier than a conventional one, it is more formal, compared to an ordinary personal letter. The customary greeting in a business letter is "Dear Sir" or "Dear Madam" . Many companies are owned and/or managed by women. If the writer is not sure whether the letter will be read by a man or a woman, it is customary to use the greeting "Dear Madam or Sir". If you are addressing a group, use "Ladies and Gentlemen". Otherwise you may use a polite description, such as "Dear friends". End the salutation with a comma or a colon. British people like comma, and American people always place a colon after a salutation. When you write a salutation, you must think of a complimentary close that can be matched with.

2.2.5 The message

The most important part of any business letter is the body of the letter, which contains the message that the writer wants to convey to the addressee. If the body of the letter is poorly written or organized, no matter how precise the forms are, this business letter is a failure. Before you begin to write, consider the following two points: What is the reason or purpose of writing this letter? What is the best way to go about it?

Since the main purpose of the letter is to convey a message, the letter should be written in a language that is easily understood. **The following serves as reminders**:

1) Study your reader's interest;
2) Adopt the right tone;
3) Write naturally and sincerely;
4) Avoid wordiness;
5) Be courteous and considerate;
6) Avoid commercial jargon;
7) Write effectively;
8) Avoid monotony;
9) Plan your letter.

Pay attention to the first and last impressions. Check your letter.

How to lay out the message? The body of a letter should start on the next line under the salutation. The left margin should be set at about an inch from the edge of the left side of the paper.

2.2.6 Complimentary Close

This is saying goodbye to your correspondent before you sign your name. The complimentary close is a greeting word or phrase to end a letter, which must also match the salutation. If the salutation is "Dear Sir", "Dear Sirs", or "Dear Madam", the matching complementary close should be "Yours Faithfully". This is formal and standard practice in Britain, while Americans use "Yours Truly" or "Sincerely Yours".

If the salutation is "Dear Mr. Wang" (somebody's name), the complimentary is "Yours sincerely", "Regards", or "Warm regards". This matches the informal salutation used between persons who know each other.

Do not use "I am", "we are", "I remain", etc. to bring a letter to the end because these phrases are old-fashioned. At one point, "Yours respectfully", was used in letters to superiors, but now it is obsolete, especially in America.

2.2.7 The signature

The signature is the signed name or mark of the person writing the letter or that of the firm he or she represents. The layout of signature is written below the complimentary close. Do not use rubber stamp, because in many countries it is a form of discourtesy. Sometimes hand written signatures can be illegible, so the name of the signer is usually typed and followed by his job title or position. **Here are some examples:**

(1) An official signing for his company

Yours faithfully,

For the Overseas Co. Ltd.

(Signature)

W. White

President

(2) A partner signing for his firm

Yours faithfully,

(Signature)

Jason Black Co.

(3) An employee with special authority to sign

Yours faithfully,

Per pro Robbins Furniture & Co.

(Signature)

Jim Li

(4) An employee without special authority to sign

Yours faithfully,

For sales manager,

(Signature)

R. Richard

2.3 Miscellaneous matters

2.3.1 References

In business communication, when a firm writes to another, each will give a reference, which includes a file number, department code or the initials of the signer followed by those of the typist of the letter. What is the function of the reference? It is linking the reply with the earlier letter. It also assures that the letter can reach the right person or department without delay. In addition, the reference enables the letter to be traced for referral.

There are three ways to lay out references. Firstly, some pre-printed letterheads provide a specific space for reference numbers. **For example**:

Your ref:

Our ref:

Secondly, the reference may form part of the first paragraph of the reply letter. **For example**:

Dear Madam,

Thank you for your letter, reference QXL/YZ of 15th October 2010.

Thirdly, the reference may be typed as a main heading. **For example**:

Dear Mr. Jones

Your ref: QXL/YZ

Thank you for your letter of 15th October 2010

2.3.2 "For the attention of "

"For the attention of" is used when the writer of a letter wants to directly address the letter to a certain person in an organization. The layout is to type it above the salutation, below the inside name and address, underlined, and centered over the body of the letter. **For example:**

The Principal

Jinan International Business School

XZ district

ZH 529000

For the attention of Dr. Huang Feng

2.3.3 Subject headings

The subject heading is the title, subtitle, or topic that begins a letter or paragraph. There are two kinds of subject headings: main headings and paragraph headings.

1) Main headings

The main heading is typed with double space below the salutation, above the body of the letter, underlined, and centered. If your correspondent uses a main heading and you are answering to that letter, you should keep the same heading. You can use the name of the product, reference number, contract number, or the quantity of the product as the main heading. Main headings do not take a full stop or any other punctuation marks. **For example:**

Dear Sirs,

Your contract No. 3456

2) Paragraph headings

The paragraph heading is a topic sentence, which is placed at the beginning of each paragraph to state the subject of the paragraph. Type the paragraph heading in block capitals; use punctuation marks such as a full stop, a colon, or a dash to emphasize the distinction between the heading and text. Since different subjects may need attention by different departments or different people, it is better to confine each letter to one subject.

2.3.4 Identification marks

The identification mark or reference notation is made up of the initials of the person who dictated the letter and those of the secretary or typist. **For example**, the manager is Angela Smith and the typist is Amy Chen, the identification marks are "AS/ac", or "AS: ac". The identification marks typed below the signature against the left margin. Between the two sets you can use a colon or a slant.

2.3.5 Enclosures

If you need to enclose something with the letter, type "Enclosure", or the short form of it "Encl." in the bottom left-hand under the identification marks. If there is more than one enclosure, use a number to indicate how many enclosures you have. **For example**, "Encl. 3".

2.3.6 Postscript

As a special device of a letter, a postscript (P. S.) has two legitimate functions. Some top managers like to add a personal touch to their typewritten letter in pen and ink. **For example**, "We appreciate what you have done for us." Some writers of sales letter often use postscript to emphasize something. **For instance**, "We will have a discussion at annual meeting on December 31." Postscript is an afterthought, which is usually a sign of poor planning.

2.3.7 Margins

The margin of a written or printed page is the empty space at the side of the page. Both left-hand and right-hand margins are generally 30mm or one inch. A brief letter can have margins as wide as 34mm. Margins contribute substantially to the visual impression a letter makes upon its reader.

2.3.8 The second page

Business letters are usually one page long, but some sales letters are complex, which need more than one page. When you have a second page, use second-page heading **For example**:

Page 2

18 December 2012
Jinan University

You can add, "to be continued" on the right hand side at the bottom of the first page. The second and succeeding pages should have the same style, size, quality, and color as the first page.

Unit 3 Addressing the Envelope

3.1 Introduction

The three most important requirements of addressing the envelope are accuracy, clarity, and good appearance. In this unit, you will learn how to accomplish all of these.

3.2 The envelope

The paper your envelope is made of should be the same quality as the paper for correspondence and memos. Remember that the quality of the paper used in your letterhead, envelopes, and business forms reflects the personality of a firm.

The standard size of business envelopes is 22cm long by 11cm wide and the standard size of letter paper is 21cm by 27.5cm; it should be folded in thirds. Smaller envelopes which are 17cm by 9cm are also used to fit special requirements, such as invitations. Before you address your envelope, choose one that is appropriate for your documents.

The return address on the envelope and the inside address on the letter should be in the same style, in the same font, **such as** Times New Roman, and use black ink. The font size should be between 10 and 14 point, depending on your choice of font and the size of the envelope. Punctuation is not usually needed except in countries such as, but not limited to, Canada and the USA, when a comma is used to separate a city and state or province. If you are using window envelopes, make sure the recipient's address can be seen clearly through the window.

Although the English and the Chinese use very different styles when addressing an envelope, the customary style and format are basically the same.

3.3 The recipient's address

The address of the receiver is normally single-spaced, and should begin one third of the way across the envelope from left to right and half way down from top to bottom. This helps to keep the important information clear and separate from other parts.

Remember to use the correspondent's full address, including the city followed by the county name and postal code or zip code as it is called in some countries. The first line of the address should list the recipient's name and title, **such as** "Mr.", "Ms.", "Dr.", or "Esq.". You also have the option to include the recipient's title beneath the name. This is typically used when addressing a company's President, CEO, CFO or other top managers. If you are sending your letter in care of another party, list that individual's name underneath the name of the recipient, with the notation "in care of" preceding the name.

Classic style formatting is conservative and formal. **For example**, do not use "No." before street numbers, but do include it when a post office box number as part of the address, **such as**: "P. O. Box No.". Another classic-style formatting rule requires that words such as "Street", "Road", and "Avenue" be spelled out in full. In modern business writing, abbreviations and signs, **such as** "#", "St.", "Rd.", and "Ave.", are allowed but should only be used when addressing correspondence going to an established client.

3.4 The return address

The return address goes on the front of the envelope in the upper left hand corner. It should include a complete address so that the letter can be returned if it is undeliverable. It should also contain the same information that you have on your business letterhead.

3.5 Other inclusions

If your letter has special delivery instructions, including airmail, certified mail or registered mail, these should be printed in all capital letters underneath the postage. If you have specific instructions for the business after delivery, including requests to keep the letter personal and confidential, print these instructions on the left side of the envelope underneath the return address and to the left side of the recipient's address.

CHINA NATIONAL IMPORT & EXPORT CORPORATION SHANGHAI BRANCH 1040 SUZHUO ROAD SHANGHAI CHINA	Stamp
	Wallace Kimber Co. 40 Nsukka Road P. O. Box 57183 Ghana
Confidential	

Unit 4 Forms of Business Letter

4.1 Introduction

There are various ways in which the component parts of a business letter can be laid out on the page. Choice of letter format is a matter of individual taste, but it is better to follow an established practice to which the business world has become accustomed. A good plan is to adopt one form of business letter format and use it for all your correspondence. The followings are some standard styles.

4.2 The block form

The main feature of the block letter is that all typing lines, including those for the date, the inside name and address, the salutation, the subject heading and the complimentary close, begin at the left-hand margin. It is very modern, now being increasingly adopted in Britain and very popular in the United States.

You can place the date in its usual position on the right, it can help to give the letter a more balanced appearance, and make it easier to find particular letters in the files. This easy-to-type letter style is becoming more and more popular and is widely used in many of today's modern offices. It is a very efficient style because everything begins at the left margins, thereby eliminating the need for tabs. Some critics say it looks somewhat crowded and imbalanced. **Here is an example:**

Herbert's Herbs
West Hill Farm
Malvern
Worcestershire
WR7 1AB

3 February 2007

Prof E. F. Gustavson

Box 1234

SE-405 999

Goteborg

Sweden

Dear Prof. Gustavson,

Thank you for your letter dated 29th January regarding our advertisement in the *Financial Times*, and for your kind remarks about our products.

I am pleased to enclose a copy of our new catalogue and look forward to receiving your order.

Warm regards,

Patricia Anderson

Marketing Manager

Telephone: 01234 567890

E-mail: marketing@ herbertsherbs. com

Website: www. herbertsherbs. com

4. 3 The indented form

The indented form requires the first word of each line to be indented one or two spaces, thus shaping the form like a "V" shape. **For example**:

3814 Oak Lane
 Dedham,
  December 8, 2010

Dr. Carolyn Brown
 Director of Research
  Evans & Associates
   Transportation Engineers
    520 Niagara Street
     Braintree, MA 021 84

Dear Dr. Brown,

Thank you very much for allowing me to tour your testing facilities. The information I gained from the tour will be of great help to me in preparing the report for my class at Marshall Institute. The tour has also given me some insight into the work I may eventually do as a laboratory technician.

I especially appreciate the time and effort Vikram Singh spent in showing me your facilities. His comments and advice were most helpful.

Again, thank you.

Sincerely,
(Signature)

4.4 The semi-block form

This style is "semi-block". The inside name and address is typed in block form, but the paragraphs forming the body of the letter are all indented six spaces. Some typists prefer a deeper indentation and may use as many as ten spaces, though six are sufficient, to show the separation of paragraphs clearly. Some parts of a letter are "block" style; some are "indented". Therefore it is called "semi-indented" style.

In general, the date appears above the inside name and address, and it can appear on the right-hand side. The salutation starts two spaces below the inside name and address, and the subject heading is centered two spaces below the salutation, and paragraphs are separated by double line-spacing. The complimentary close is typed in the center of the typing line, with the designation similarly centered. You can place the complimentary close to the right of center rather than in the center.

Hongxin's Department Store
4507 Shanghai Road
Nanjing, Jiangsu 210047

June 7, 2012
Ketchum Collection Agency
1267 Hollywood Boulevard
Los Angeles, California 91404
U. S. A.

Ladies and Gentlemen:

Subject: Mr. Gary Daniels, Account # 69 112 003

We would like to turn over to your services the account of Mr. Gray Daniels, 4441 Natick Avenue, Sherman Oak, California 91418. The balance on Mr. Daniels' account, $829.95, is now 120 days past due; although we have sent him four statements and five letters, we have been unable to collect his debt.

Mr. Daniels is employed by West Coast Furniture Showrooms, Inc. He banks at the Natick Avenue branch of Third National City Bank and has been a customer of ours for four years. We have enclosed his file for your reference.

We are confident that we can rely on Ketchum as we have in the past. Please let us know if there is any further information we can furnish you.

Sincerely,
Hongxin's Department Store
Mary Zhang
Credit Manager

4.5 The simplified form

Designed by the Administrative Management Society, this style is the same as full-blocked, with these exceptions:

No salutation or complimentary closing is used, and an entirely capitalized subject line must be used. The signer's identification is typed in all capitals. Lists are indented five spaces unless numbered or lettered in which cases they are blocked with no periods after the numbers or letters. This style is extremely efficient because it requires less time to type than other styles. However, it is somehow impersonal. For this reason, the reader's name should be mentioned at least once in the body of the letter.

NORP

NATIONAL ORGANIZATION OF RETIRED PERSONS

Freeport High School, Freeport, Vermont 66622

October 14, 2010

Ms. Iva Stravinsky

Attorney-at-Law

200 Center Street

Freeport, Vermont 66621

Thank you for offering to give a presentation about "Proposed Changes in the Financing of Medicare" at our club. The members of the Freeport chapter of the National Organization of Retired Persons would indeed be interested in this topic. I accept your offer to address our club.

The NORP meets every Tuesday at 8 p.m. in the auditorium of Freeport High School. Our meeting programs have already been established through November 20. I will call you in a few days to schedule a date for your lecture on any Tuesday of your choice after November 20.

Ms. Stravinsky, the membership, and I look forward to your lecture on such an important topic.

HENRY PURCELL, PRESIDENT

HP/bm

Studying effective business writing is a practical and useful skill that is necessary in establishing and maintaining a good relationship with your customers. It is also the study of cultural styles that will aid in developing language effectively.

Unit 5 Establishing Business Relations

5.1 Introduction

Writing a letter of establishing business relations is the first step to start a business. In general, a foreign-trade firm needs extensive business connections to maintain or expand its business. One of the methods is to write a letter to establish business relations. Therefore writing business letters is an important undertaking in the field of foreign trade. The importer is usually in one country and the exporter in another. They are separated sometimes by thousands of miles. Writing letters to new companies to set up a business connection is the first step in foreign trade.

Writing a good business letter is as vitally important for new firms as well as it is for well-established firms that wish to increase their business scope and production. There are four major parts in this unit: channels you can use to get information, the types of letters for establishing business connections, the letter contents and some sample letters.

5.2 Information channel

When your firm wants to open up a market to sell to or buy something from firms in foreign countries, you must first find out whom you are going to deal with. You should know the name of the company, the person who is in charge of the business, their business scope, and their interest, etc. Such information is available through **the following channels**:

1) Chambers of Commerce in foreign cities and countries;

2) Banks;

3) Trade Directories;

4) Chinese Commercial Counselor's Office in foreign countries;

5) Competitors;

6) Advertisements;

7) Employees of the company's subsidiaries or branches;

8) Market investigations.

And there are some other channels, such as attendance at export commodity fairs, trade delegations or other business groups, an introduction from your business connections.

5.3 Types of letters

Use the sources above, research the names and addresses of firms and compile a list of companies to start sending letters, circulars, brochures, and catalogue. The purpose of writing a letter is to establish business relations, and it is also the first time you ask for information, which is why it is called "first inquiry". Usually, you can start the letter by informing the receiver how you have heard about him or his business. Next, give some general information about the products your business handles. If you intend to buy for import, you may also make request for catalogue, samples, price lists, etc. Close the letter by expressing your expectations for cooperation and an early reply. You should state simply, clearly, and concisely what you need to buy or what you can sell.

5.4 Letter content

The contents of a letter to establish business relations must **include**:

1) The source of your information—where and how you know something about your reader;

2) Your intention—why you are writing;

3) The business scope of your firm—which is introducing yourself;

4) Reference to the firm's financial position and integrity.

If you receive a letter in this nature, it must be answered without delay, and with courtesy and respect. This will create goodwill and leave a good impression on the reader.

Before a writer corresponds to a new customer, he should conduct a credit investigation including: capital and financial condition; capacity and business activity; character, honesty, and integrity.

Business connections are very valuable to firms engaged in foreign trade. Therefore, traders must not only do everything possible to solidify their business relationship with existing clients, but they also need to search for new connections to develop.

Letters that are intended to establish business relations must be friendly, helpful, and cordial. The first step is to state your objectives in a simple opening sentence, expressing your desire to establish a business relationship. The second step is to think from your reader's point of view: put yourself in the shoes of the people who will be reading your message. Use language you think your reader will understand clearly. The third step is to select the appropriate style to present your information.

5.5 Sample letters

(1)

Dear Sirs,

We obtained your address from the Commercial Counselor at your embassy in London. We are interested in your products and would like to establish business relationship with your company.

Our company is well connected with the major light industrial product dealers. As a result, we feel confident we can sell large quantities of Chinese goods if your prices are competitive.

The Bank of England, London, can confirm our business references. Please forward us all the necessary information regarding your products for export.

Yours truly,

Embassy/Dealer/Offer/Standing

(2)

Dear Sir or Madam,

Messrs Anderson and Co., Rotterdam, has referred your company to us and we are writing today in the hope of establishing a business relationship with your company. We have been importers of Arts and Crafts for many years. Currently, we are interested in Chinese Arts and Crafts and would like to receive your catalogue and price lists.

If your prices are reasonable, you can expect a business contract to materialize.

We look forward to receiving your early reply.

Yours faithfully,

(Signature)

(**3**)

Dear Ms. Smith,

Your company has been referred to us as prospective buyers of Chinese cotton goods by Messrs Freeman and Co. Ltd, New York. As this item falls within the scope of our business ventures, we would like to establish a business relationship with you at your earliest convenience.

To give you a general idea of the various kinds of cotton goods now available for export, we have enclosed a brochure and our price list. Quotations and sample books will be sent to you upon receipt of your specific inquiry.

Yours faithfully,

(Signature)

5.6 Word study

(1) **Chambers of Commerce**: an association of business persons and merchants for the promotion of commercial interests in the community.

(2) **Trade Directory**: a book containing an alphabetical or classified listing of names, addresses, and other data, such as telephone numbers, of specific persons, groups, or firms.

(3) **Counselor**: a person who gives counsel; an adviser.

(4) **Delegation**: a person or group of persons officially elected or appointed to represent a group or person.

(5) **Connection**: a person, especially one of influence or position, with whom one is associated, as by kinship, interests in common, or marriage.

(6) **Scope**: the area covered by a given activity or subject.

(7) **Integrity**: steadfast adherence to a strict moral or ethical code.

(8) **Embassy**: a building containing the offices of an ambassador and staff.

(9) **Dealer**: one that is engaged in buying and selling.

(10) **Offer**: a proposal that if accepted constitutes a legally binding contract.

(11) **Standing**: status with respect to rank, reputation, or position in society or a profession.

(12) **Establish**: to set up, begin, create.

(13) **Messrs**: American English means plural form of Mr. used especially in the names of companies.

(14) **Co.**: abbreviation of the word "company".

(15) **Importer**: a company or country that imports.

(16) **Appreciate**: recognize and enjoy.

(17) **Catalogue**: a list of places, news, objects, goods etc., often with information about them, put in a special order so that they can be found easily.

(18) **Quotations**: the calculated cost of a piece of work.

(19) **Materialize (of something planned or expected)**: to become real or actual. *E. g.* He always wanted a large family, but his hopes never materialized.

5.7 Useful sentences

(1) We have heard from the China Council for the Promotion of International Trade that you are in the market for electric appliances.

(2) Messrs. J. Smith & Co. Inc. of New York has given us your contact information as one of the leading importers of light industrial products in your country.

(3) On the recommendation of ... Co. Ltd., we are contacting you to establish a business relationship.

(4) We understand you are potential buyers of Chinese ..., which is a product we produce.

(5) We would like to introduce ourselves to you with the intent of building a business relationship with your firm.

(6) Specializing in the export of Chinese cotton ..., we would like to establish a trade agreement with you to provide this line.

(7) We are interested in the possibility of establishing ... sources of crude oil from your country.

(8) Because we are closely connected with reliable wholesalers, we have the

resources to establish a substantial import business with you.

(9) Please submit full specifications of your . . . together with terms of payment and discount rates.

(10) Please furnish us with your samples of rayon handkerchiefs that closely match the design and quality of those enclosed.

(11) In order to give you an idea of various qualities of handicrafts we carry, we are happy to send you a variety of sample books for your perusal.

(12) Your letter addressed to . . . was forwarded to us for our attention. Our firm exclusively handles the export of this product.

(13) The China Council for the Promotion of International Trade in Beijing has referred your letter of . . . to our corporate office in Beijing to establish business relations.

(14) We would be pleased if you would respond to our request at your earliest convenience.

(15) Having obtained your name and address from International Business School Jinan University. . .

(16) We are one of the representative importers/exporters. . .

(17) Your name was given to us by . . .

(18) If we can enter into business relation with you . . .

(19) We are one of the leading importers/exporters of . . .

(20) We enjoy an excellent reputation. . .

Unit 6 Inquiries and Replies

6.1 Introduction

Inquiries for information about goods or services are sent and received in business all the time. In the international trade, a buyer usually makes an inquiry to invite a quotation or offer from a seller in order to buy a certain commodity or obtain a specific service.

You should reply the letter as soon as possible, answering the questions, supplying the information and/or materials, offering special help and try to satisfy the needs of those who make the requests. This unit discusses the types of inquiries, the content of the letter, and how to write an inquiry and make a reply.

6.2 Types of inquiry

There are two kinds of inquiry: general inquiry and specific inquiry. In a general inquiry, a company states clearly all the information they need: general information about your company, a catalogue, a price list, and samples or sample books. In a specific inquiry, they point out what certain products they want. They may ask for a catalogue, a price list, a sample, or ask for a quote that concerns a certain product.

In foreign trade, the buyers ask for some information such as price, catalogue, delivery date, and so on. Inquiries may be sent by mail, email, telephone, fax, or handed to the suppliers through personal contact.

6.3 Responses to inquiries

The supplier's reply must provide the customer with the correct information and answer all questions. The supplier should always be polite when writing a reply. It can be an expression of appreciation to an established customer or thanks to a new customer or potential buyer with the hope of establishing or maintaining a lasting and friendly business relationship. Even if the goods ordered are not presently available or some special terms cannot be granted, the supplier should never offend the customer or they may lose future business.

In a reply letter writing, an effective beginning and ending are always highly desired. They not only indicate your high efficiency of doing business, but also have psychological advantages. Therefore, the opening should contain no more than three or four lines, be positive and direct, and convey information clearly and concisely. **For example:**

(1) I am writing to reply your inquiry about...
(2) Thank you for your inquiry of...
(3) In reply to your letter of... I am very pleased to inform you...

After the opening the writer proceeds with the main objective of the inquiry and provides information with commonly used words. **For example:**

(1) We would like you to know...
(2) I am very pleased to inform you...

The ending should be brief and hold the reader's attention, leaving no question about what to do next. The ending restates the main purpose and summarizes any proposals. **For example:**

(1) We hope our catalogue and samples will reach you in good time.
(2) As a result of the market showing an upward tendency, it would be profitable for you to place an order without delay.

Finally, the ending should urge the reader to take action. **For example:**

(1) Our products are selling very fast; I suggest you place your order as soon as possible.

(2) I hope you are satisfied with our answer.

Inquiries and replies are important steps in the process of concluding a deal. They are indispensable to reach an agreement. Writing good inquiries and replies produces goodwill and potential business. To become proficient in your writing skills, a person needs much practice and study of effective sample letters.

6.4 Notes

In writing inquiries and replies to them, a direct approach is advised. In an inquiry the customer comes straight to the point from the beginning of the letter. The customer then states a necessary and explicit explanation of why he made the inquiry. The customer directly calls the supplier's attention to details and asks for a prompt reply. Occasionally, a customer prefers to begin an inquiry with some background information to show courtesy and respect to the supplier, particularly for the first few inquiries. The first inquiry is written by a customer to a supplier that the customer has not previously dealt with. In this case, the customer may mention how they obtained information about the supplier, and give some information about their own business. The customer should always remember that only necessary background and explanatory information is suitable, and anything else is of secondary importance.

When you are making inquiries, you should consider carefully region or regions your inquiries are sent and how many suppliers are to be approached in that same region. If you don't consider this information, it could produce an adverse effect on your future transactions. Pay great attention to the religions and customs of another country to prevent offending the suppliers. There is no need for long, overly polite phrases and humbleness. Many firms use a printed inquiry form instead of a letter.

To receive quick attention, inquiries should be addressed to the company. If you address your inquiries to an individual, your letter may go unopened if the individual is out of the office. If you make a mistake and address your letter to the wrong person, this will also cause delays and confusion.

If goods mentioned in the inquiry are currently out of stock, the supplier should inform the inquirer when they will be available. To create a good impression, take this opportunity to introduce other products as possible substitutes, which could result in additional business. In conclusion, inquires should be brief, specific, courteous and reasonable. The replies should be prompt, courteous, and helpful.

6.5 Sample letters

(1)

Gentlemen:

We learn from ABC & Co.. Ltd., New York that you are a leading exporter in your country.

We are, at present, very much interested in importing your goods and would appreciate your sending us catalogue, sample books or even samples if possible.

Please give us detailed information of CIF Guangzhou prices, discounts, and terms of payment.

We hope this will be a good start for a long and profitable business relation.

Yours truly,

(Signature)

(2)

Dear Sirs,

We are desirous of having your lowest quotation for the article on the terms and conditions mentioned below, to which your prompt attention is requested.

Description of article: Tin foil sheets

Quantity required: About 50 long tons of 2,240 pounds.

Price: CFR Shanghai, including cost of suitable packing for export.

Terms of payment: By irrevocable L/C to be opened in your favor ten days after your acceptance of the order.

Time of shipment: June/July, 2003

We trust that you will send us your reply by return.

Yours faithfully,

(Signature)

(3)

August 14, 2002

Dear Sirs,

We are interested to buy large quantities of Iron Nails of all sizes. We would be grateful if you would give us a quotation per ton CFR Lagos, Nigeria. We would also appreciate if you could forward samples and/or catalogue to us.

We used to purchase this article from other sources, however we now prefer to buy from your company. We understand you are able to supply large quantities at a more attractive price, and we have great confidence in the quality of Chinese products.

We look forward to hearing from you by return mail.

Yours faithfully,

(Signatwe)

(4)

Gentlemen:

We welcome your inquiry of March 21st and thank you for your interest in our export commodities. We are enclosing some copies of our illustrated catalogue and a price list giving the details you asked for. Also under separate cover, we are sending you some samples which will show you clearly the quality and craftsmanship of our products. We trust that when you see them you will agree that our products appeal to the most selective buyers. We offer a discount according to the quantity ordered. As to the terms of payment, we usually require L/C payable by sight draft.

Thank you again for your interest in our products. We are looking forward to your order and assure you that it will receive our prompt and careful attention.

Yours truly,

(Signature)

6.6 Word study

(1) **Commodity**: an article of trade or commerce, especially an agricultural or mining product that can be transported.

(2) **Illustrate**: to provide (a publication) with explanatory or decorative features.

(3) **Sight draft (abbr. SD)**: draft or bill that is payable on demand or upon presentation.

(4) **Tin foil sheets**: a very thin bendable sheet of shiny metal, used as a protective wrapping, especially wrapping or covering food before cooking it.

(5) **Terms and conditions**: the conditions of an agreement; the stated conditions of a contract concerning payment, prices, etc. which are necessary in order for business to happen or exist.

(6) **Attention**: particular care or consideration given to something, specifically with the aim of taking action.

(7) **Description**: to say what something is like, for example, the name of the commodity.

(8) **Long ton**: unit of weight; long ton: 1016 kg; short ton: 907kg; ton: 1000kg.

(9) **In your favor**: you are the receiver, beneficiary; the receiver of a benefit or advantage.

(10) **Irrevocable**: cannot be changed once it has been started.

(11) **By return**: by return of post, Britain English "by the next post" or American English "by return mail".

(12) **Iron**: a very common and useful metal which is a simple substance. It is used in the making of steel, and is found in very small quantities in certain foods and in the blood.

(13) **Nail**: a thin pointed piece of metal.

(14) **Quantities**: the fact of being measurable; amount.

(15) **Used to**: something that always or regularly happened in the past.

(16) **Prefer to**: to choose one thing or action over another.

(17) **Prompt**: performed with little or no delay. *E. g.* A prompt reply to my letter; prompt obedience.

(18) **Appeal**: attractiveness that interests or pleases or stimulates. *E. g.* His smile was part of his appeal to her.

(19) **CIF**: stands for Cost, Insurance, and Freight (named port of destination), which mean the seller has responsibility to arrange and pay for the shipment of the goods to the port of destination and provide insurance coverage at his own expense. The risk of loss or damage to the goods is transferred from the seller to the buyer once the goods are loaded on board the ship at the named port of shipment.

6. 7 Useful sentences

(1) We are interested in . . .

(2) As advertised recently in . . .

(3) We have noticed your advertisement in . . . and would like you to send us your catalogue and the price list of your products.

(4) I understand you are the manufacturer of . . . and I would like to receive your current catalogue.

(5) We would be grateful if you could send us some samples.

(6) Please send me the illustrated copy of your current catalogue, price list and tell us the earliest possible date for delivery.

(7) Please tell us how long this price list will be valid.

(8) We would appreciate you sending us your catalogue of . . . and tell us the best discount you can give us.

(9) Under these circumstances, please indicate whether you will offer us a special discount.

(10) If you can supply suitable goods, we may place regular orders for large quantities of . . .

(11) We have an urgent need for your products and would like to know if you have a large quantity of goods in stock.

(12) We trust you will favor us with a prompt reply.

(13) We thank you for your letter of . . .

(14) We are in receipt of your letter dated . . .

(15) Thank you for your letter of . . . As requested, we have enclosed . . .

(16) Thank you for your inquiry dated . . . regarding . . .

(17) In reply to your letter of . . . , I am very pleased to inform you . . .

(18) In reply to your request of . . . , we are sending by separate post . . .

(19) You will find details of our terms and a price list printed on the inside front cover of the catalogue.

(20) Today, we sent you an array of samples specially selected for you.

(21) Our price list is enclosed and shows details of our conditions and terms of trading.

(22) If you need more information, just write to . . .

(23) We look forward to receiving a trial order from you soon.

(24) Please fax us your quotation at your convenience.

(25) We would appreciate a quick response to quoting export trading.

(26) Please let us know on what terms and conditions you can deliver the televisions.

(27) We believe that there is a declining market in this field; we hope you can give us a reply as soon as possible.

(28) We would be pleased to discuss the possibility of having our products distributed in your country.

(29) We would be happy to arrange a meeting at a mutually agreeable time.

(30) Thank you for expressing interest in our company.

(31) One of our business friends, Mr. Carlson, informed us that your company is a major manufacturer of pure cotton shirts in all sizes for middle-aged women.

Unit 7 Quotations

7. 1 Introduction

A quotation is a reply to an inquiry. It is an offer in simple form including a notice of the price of certain goods being sold, but not in a strict legal sense. When a manufacturer or seller prepares to export, he quotes the customer the price of the goods ordered on the receipt of the inquiry. The success of the business depends on whether the correct quotation is made or not.

Sellers will send a quotation to buyers in response to their inquiries. A quotation will include all necessary information requested in the inquiry. It is a promise to supply goods according to the terms stated. The prospective buyer is under no obligation to buy the goods when a quote is requested, and the seller is not bound to sell the goods he has previously quoted if he later decides not to do so. A quotation is not legally binding although it contains some qualifying words that function as firm offers do. There are several questions discussed in this unit: the contents of a quotation, notes to write, and sample letters.

7. 2 Letter content

A quotation generally has six parts, however, not every part is necessary each time a quote is given.

1) An expression of thanks for the inquiry;
2) Details of prices, discounts, and terms of payments;
3) A statement or clear indication of what the prices cover;
4) An estimated date of delivery or estimated time of shipment;
5) The period for which the quotation is valid;
6) Your hope that the quotation will be accepted.

7.3 Notes

Quotation letters convey information of sales terms. Their writing usually takes the same direct approach as is used in an inquiry. A good offer is written clearly, concisely, and to the point. Start the letter with your reason or purpose for writing; thank the customer for their request. **For example**:

(1) Thank you for your letter of... asking for a quotation...
(2) In reply to your letter of...
(3) It is our pleasure to offer you...
(4) We are pleased to submit our quote...

In the body of the letter, you confirm the availability of your stock and state all the terms and conditions in a complete, clear, and definite way. In case the inquiry results in a quotation, the terms must be stated accurately. **For example**:

(1) The following quotation is subject to your final confirmation:...
(2) We have the pleasure of offering you... we are pleased to present a quote as follows:...
(3) We offer you goods of the highest quality with unusually generous terms.
(4) We look forward to your prompt acceptance accompanied by your order.

To end your letter, express your hope that the quotation or offer is satisfactory to the correspondent and will be accepted.

7.4 Sample letters

(1)

THE BRITAIN TRADING CO., LTD.
No. 20 Wright Street
London, England
E-mail: bri@handbag.com
2nd July, 2004

Dear Sirs,

We thank you very much for your letter of June 30, asking for information on our leather handbags, and your request for our latest catalogue. As per your request, enclosed is our latest price list for this month. A full range of handbag samples have been sent to you today, and we are confident that, after examining them, you will see that the quality and the prices of the goods we offer compare favorably to any others on the market.

We can assure you that these goods are very popular in western markets, based on our experience. We are continually issuing new designs and would be delighted to send you samples if you start ordering from us on a regular basis. When you place an order for more than 500 pieces, we would give you a special discount of 5% if paid within 10 days of our invoice.

We hope that this will be the beginning of a long-term business relationship with your company.

Yours faithfully,

THE BRITAIN TRADING CO., LTD
(SIGNATURE)
E. Thompson
President

(**2**)

Dear Sirs,

We received your letter dated August 18, and are delighted to learn of your interest in our vacuum cleaners, models NW20 and NW22. enclosed, and you will find our conditions of sales and payment terms.

We have reviewed your proposal to place an order for a guaranteed minimum number of our new products in return for a special allowance. After considering it carefully, we feel it would be better to offer you a special allowance on the following sliding-scale basis:

On purchases exceeding an annual total of:

US $20,000 but not exceeding US $30,000 ………………………… 2%

US $30,000 but not exceeding US $40,000 ………………………… 3%

US $40, 000 and above 4%
No special allowance could be given on annual total purchase below US $20, 000.

We feel this arrangement would be beneficial to both of us. We would be pleased to learn that you accept our proposal, and we look forward to working with you.

Yours faithfully,
(Signature)

(3)
Dear Sirs,
We thank you for your inquiry of August 22 and are pleased to send you our quotation for the goods you required as follows:
Commodity: "White Rabbit" Brand Woolen Mixed Blanket No. 33.
Size: 74 × 84 in
Weight: 4lbs
Color: yellow, brown, green assortment
Quantity: 1, 000pcs
Price: US $40. 00 per piece CIF Montreal
Shipment: October
You are cordially invited to take advantage of this attractive offer. We are anticipating a large order from the United States, and that will cause a sharp rise in price.
We look forward to receive your order.
Yours faithfully,
(Signature)

(4)
Dear Sirs,

Re: 5900 tons Shandong Groundnuts

We acknowledge receipt of your letter of Sept. 15, 2006, inquiring about our groundnuts. In reply, we make you the following quotation, subject to our final confirmation:

(1) Commodity: Shandong Groundnuts, handpicked, ungraded.

(2) Quantity: 59 tons.

(3) (Unit) Price: US $... net per ton CFR Copenhagen.

(4) Shipment: During Nov. /Dec. this year, from Guangzhou.

(5) Payment: By irrevocable L/C payable against drafts at sight.

(6) Insurance: F. P. A

As usual, we do not allow any discount, as business has already been done at the above price and Shandong Groundnuts are selling fast at present. If you find the above terms acceptable, please cable us with confirmation.

Yours faithfully,

(Signature)

7.5 Word study

(1) **Confident**: having or marked by confidence or assurance. *E. g.* a confident speaker; a confident reply; confident of fulfillment; His manner is more confident these days.

(2) **Compare**: examine and note the similarities or differences of sth. *E. g.* John compared his haircut to his friend's; We compared notes after we both saw the movie.

(3) **Issue**: bring out an official document such as a warrant.

(4) **Discount**: the act of reducing the selling price of merchandise.

(5) **Invoice**: an itemized statement of money owed for goods shipped or services rendered.

(6) **Model**: a simplified description of a complex entity or process. *E. g.* The computer program was based on a model of the circulatory and respiratory systems.

(7) **Allowance**: an amount added or deducted on the basis of qualifying circumstances. *E. g.* an allowance for profit.

(8) **Proposal**: something proposed (such as a plan or suggestion).

(9) **Rabbit**: a burrowing mammal with long ears, soft fur, and a short tail.

(10) **Woolen**: made or consisting of wool.

(11) **Lb**: means pound, which is a unit of weight equivalent to 16 ounces.

(12) **Groundnut**: peanut or monkey-nut is a nut that grows in a shell under the ground, and can be eaten.

(13) **Confirmation**: to give support or certainty to (a fact, belief, statement),

for example by providing more proof or by stating that something is true or correct.

(14) **Ungraded**: not separated into levels or rank of quality.

(15) **Unit**: an amount or quantity used as a standard of measurement.

(16) **Draft**: a written order for money to be paid by a bank, especially from one bank to another.

(17) **Insurance**: agreement by contract to pay money to someone, if something, such as illness, death, or an accident, happens to them.

(18) **Cable**: to send something or tell someone by telegram.

(19) **Cordially**: in a hearty manner. *E. g.* We welcomed her cordially; Cordially yours.

(20) **Anticipating**: regard something as probable or likely. *E. g.* The meteorologists are expecting rain for tomorrow.

(21) **Assortment**: a collection containing a variety of things.

(22) **Delighted**: filled with wonder and delight.

7.6 Useful sentences

(1) Thank you for your interest in our products...

(2) We were pleased to receive your letter of inquiry about our products.

(3) We thank you for your inquiry of... and are pleased to enclose our quote as follows: ...

(4) In reference to your inquiry of..., we shall gladly supply... at the price of...

(5) We are pleased to offer the following: ...

(6) We are pleased to send you our enclosed quotation for...

(7) All quotations are subject to our final confirmation.

(8) We trust you will find our quotation satisfactory and look forward to receiving your order.

(9) In reply to your letter of... and subject to our final confirmation, we have the pleasure of offering the captioned goods as follows: ...

(10) We are making you the following offer.

(11) This is a firm offer, subject to the receipt of your reply to us before January 30.

(12) It is our pleasure to make you this special offer, subject to our final confirmation.

(13) We will keep this offer open until the end of this month.

(14) To take advantage of this offer, you must respond to it by January 30.

(15) We trust you will find our prices competitive and we look forward to receiving your order.

(16) We kept the price close to our costs of production, hoping you will give us your reply at your earliest convenience.

(17) No other buyers bid higher than the price we quoted you last week.

(18) You will see that our quotation compares favorably with those you can get elsewhere.

(19) This competitive quotation is based on a strengthening market.

Unit 8 Sales Letters

8.1 Introduction

There are two types of business letters in foreign trade communications, one is letters of establishing business relations and another type is known as sales letters, whose purpose is also to increase business and to persuade the buyer to buy their products or services.

A sales letter is a piece of direct mail that is designed to persuade the reader to purchase a particular product or service in the absence of a salesman. It has been defined as "a form of direct mail in which an advertiser sends a letter to a potential customer".

The modern trend in writing a sales letter is making the letters more personal. A good sales letter-writer tries to represent the offer from the point of view of the buyer, not the seller. This unit discusses the types of sales letters, notes to write, and sample letters.

8.2 Types of sales letters

There are several types of sales letters: the reviver letter, the circular and the follow-up letter.

1) The reviver letter

A "reviver" is a letter which is not used to acquire new customers, but to retain or reclaim old ones, such as old partners and old customers. Reviver letters are written when the writer has had no substantial business interactions with the receiver for a long time. The seller writes the letter with the intention to get the buyer's cooperation. Such letters usually contain **the following elements**:

(1) A review of their past cooperative relationship;

(2) Additional favorable comments on the goods;

(3) To offer a generous discount or favorable terms;

(4) To express the hope of receiving a new order.

2) The circular

Sales letters and reviver letters are often written in the form of a "circular". But most people like to throw them away without reading them; therefore when you write a circular, **the following rules should be kept in mind**:

(1) Businessmen nowadays are very busy and prefer to receive short letters. So make your message short.

(2) Arouse the reader's interest in the first paragraph.

(3) Give the letter an attractive appearance and make it personal and friendly.

3) The follow-up letters

The third type of sales letters is "follow-up" letter, which is the letter that follows the quotation that the firm has made already. It will express regret or surprise that no order has been received and may ask the reasons. You can put new comments and arguments in the follow-up letter to persuade your reader again to buy your products. The letter ends with the repeated hope that the customer will take advantage of the offer. Some follow-up letters are quite short, you should make it as personal as possible; it will be more effective.

8. 3 Notes

When writing a sales letter, the seller should try to present the offer from the point of view of the buyer; not the seller. Writing sales letters is one of the routine duties of a salesperson. A good sales letter will create a positive base, and increase your opportunity for business. Remember the generals sales strategy: analyze the products, find the prospects, choose the appeal, and identify the specific goal.

Sales letters are persuasive messages. Persuasion means a process of changing people's attitudes or influencing their actions, now or in the future. The purpose of a sales letter is to create a customer's interest in your product or service, and to turn a potential customer into an actual customer. To write an effective sales letter, it is important that you prepare yourself well. First, you must know your product thoroughly. Second, you should learn as much about your customers as possible. Third, you'll need to learn about your competitors' products. **The followings are the**

principles of sales writing:

1) Attract the readers' attention.
2) Stimulate the reader's interest in the product.
3) Stress the benefits of the offer to the reader.
4) Convince the reader to act immediately.

The promotion letter is another way to build buyers' interest in a new product or service. Promotions differ from sales letters in format and are written not to individuals but to a wide range of potential customers.

The four principles of writing an effective sales letter are true for promotion letters as well, but the format of the promotion letter is less restrictive. The body of the promotion letter is often broken up with headings, underlined or in capital letters or both. This allows you to highlight the major points of your sales message.

Understanding that people are motivated by needs, advertising researchers have come up with long lists of appeals that make people take notice. But people have different needs and that is why they respond to any given message in a different way. So you should analyze your readers, consider their needs, hopes, and problems, and then construct a letter to meet their needs.

There are three "Don'ts" in writing a sales letter:

1) A promise made in a sales letter is held to be binding according to the law of some countries, especially some developing countries. Therefore, do not use contract forms or contract patterns when you write a sales letter.
2) Do not exaggerate the fact, especially about the price, quality, or product functions. For example, "Our price of our product is the lowest in this city." So do not make a false statement in a sales letter.
3) Do not use a person's name or other identity in a sales letter without permission. For example, do not write "Andrea Bochelli loves our product", if he does not know anything about it, or do not ask permission to use his name. This is an invasion of privacy; you might be taken to court for it.

8. 4 Sample letters

(1) An introduction letter

Dear Mrs. Jane Robert,

Re: Excellent Opportunity to Buy Sanitary Wares

We have learned from Flying Trading Co., Ltd. that you are setting up a new office building. We believe you will benefit from Red Pearl, a major producer of high/medium-end sanitary and bathroom equipment.

We develop products with experienced engineers and marketing professionals to ensure that what we offer to customers is not only aesthetically appealing, but also functionally superior. Our products are popular with customers in over 20 countries and regions.

We invite you to visit our facilities and see firsthand the design, craftsmanship, and technology of our company and to see why we stand above the competition in delivering our line of products and supporting services.

We enclose an illustrated catalogue of our latest products for your reference. We look forward to your early reply. If you have any question about our products, please call our toll-free number at 0086-800-850-6688.

Sincerely,

(Signature)

(2) A reviver (in e-mail form)

To: Peter@aol. com

Subject: A Generous Discount

Dear Peter,

We have noticed that your revered company has been a valuable customer of ours for the last three years. We have received regular orders from you for large quantities of ceramic products. However, we are disappointed that we haven't had the pleasure of hearing from you during the last six months.

We think you may be interested to know that recently we have developed many new products. In order to promote the sales of these products, we are extending a generous discount to our valued buyers on the prevailing price of US $20. 50 per set CIF San Francisco. The discounts are as follows:

Tableware Art. No. Y6688

3% discount for an order of 1000 sets to 1999 sets.

6% discount for an order of 2000 sets to 2999 sets.

9% discount for an order of 3000 sets and above.

Enclosed please find the new design for this item. Our offer is subject to your reply reaching us on or before September 30.

At the present, our discount on new products is given only to established customers. We hope that you will consider our offer.

We look forward to a favorable response at your earliest convenience.

Sincerely,

Henry Cai,

General Manager

Shanghai Huali Imp. & Exp. Co. , Ltd

Rm. 606 Plaza Building, Fax: 86-21-642578 * *

1302 Meilong Road, 200237 Tel: 86-21-642578 * *

Shanghai, People's Republic of China

E-mail: huali88@ alibab. com. cn

(3) A follow-up letter

Feixiang International Trading Co. , Ltd.

45 Zhongshan Road, Xiamen, Fujian, China

Tel: (0592) 59876543 Fax: (0592) 5987556

P. O. Box: 361000

E-mail: Feixiang66@ alibaba. com. cn

September 20, 2012

Mr. Albert Woodrow

Sales manager

Horizon Logistics Corporation

Melbourne, Australia

Dear Mr. Woodrow,

On September 10, we replied to your inquiry for air-conditioners. As of today, we have not had the pleasure of hearing from you. We would like to know if we could help you in any way to make your decision sooner.

Perhaps the enclosed copy of our recently published booklet can help you to decide sooner. The booklet shows our latest wide range of household electric appliances, including microwave ovens, refrigerators, and air-conditioners. They are all recommended as sales-ready for their durability and energy-saving properties.

If any of the items illustrated in the booklet interests you, please do not hesitate to let us know. We will send you pricing information upon receipt of your detailed requirements. We sincerely hope we can initiate a sales transaction with you in the near future.

Regards,

(Signature)

8.5 Word study

(1) **Sanitary**: free from filth and pathogens. *E. g.* sanitary conditions for preparing food; a sanitary washroom.

(2) **Aesthetically**: in a tasteful way. *E. g.* This building is aesthetically very pleasing.

(3) **Ceramic**: an artifact made of hard brittle material produced from nonmetallic minerals by firing at high temperatures.

(4) **Prevail**: be valid, applicable, or true.

(5) **Convenience**: the state of being suitable or opportune. *E. g.* Chairs arranged for his own convenience.

(6) **Booklet**: a small book usually having a paper cover.

(7) **Appliance**: durable goods for home or office use.

(8) **Refrigerator**: an appliance in which food can be stored at low temperatures to retain freshness.

(9) **Revere**: regard with feelings of respect and reverence; consider hallowed or exalted or be in awe of. *E. g.* Fear God as your father or we revere genius.

(10) **Toll**: value measured by what must be given or done or undergone to obtain something; or a fee charged for the use of roads or bridges.

(11) **Promote**: make publicity for; try to sell (a product). *E. g.* The salesman is aggressively promoting the new computer model. The company is heavily promoting their new laptops.

(12) **Logistics**: handling an operation that involves providing labor and materials as needed.

(13) **Durability**: permanence by virtue of the power to resist stress or force. *E. g.* They advertised the durability of their products.

(14) **Transaction**: the act of conducting business within or between groups (as carrying on commercial activities). *E. g.* No transactions are possible without him.

(15) **Superior**: one of greater rank or station or quality.

(16) **Craftsmanship**: skill in an occupation or trade. *E. g.* a very high standard of craftsmanship.

(17) **Extend**: make available; provide. *E. g.* extend a loan; The bank offers a good extend on new mortgages.

(18) **Tableware**: articles for use at the table.

8.6 Useful sentences

(1) We have learned from Flying Trading Co., Ltd. that you are setting up a new office building.

(2) We have enclosed an illustrated catalogue of our latest products for your reference and look forward to your early reply.

(3) We noted that your esteemed company has been a valuable customer of ours during the last three years.

(4) You may be interested to know that recently we have developed many new products.

(5) Presently, our discount on new products is given only to established customers. We hope that you will take this into consideration.

(6) We look forward to your favorable reply at your earliest convenience.

(7) If any of the items illustrated in the booklet interests you, please do not hesitate to let us know. We will offer you a quotation upon receipt of your

detailed requirements. We sincerely hope to do business with you in the near future.

(8) Would you like to reduce your production costs?

(9) Imagine how enjoyable it will be when you stand before class using our new computer.

(10) If you are interested in our service, our booklet can give you more information.

(11) We learned through a business committee you might be interested in our products and services.

(12) We are pleased to offer you an 8% discount if you buy more than 1,000 pieces.

(13) Do not miss great opportunities to study abroad through my agency.

(14) Wearing our new style dresses is a wonderful way to highlight how beautiful you are!

(15) In order to popularize these products, all the catalogue prices are subjected to a special discount of 10% during this month only.

(16) The high quality of our products is well known and universally acknowledged.

(17) If our business range can meet your needs, do not hesitate to contact us.

(18) If you are interested in our product, we will be most happy to assist you in any way we can.

(19) To celebrate the opening of our store, we will allow you a special discount of 10%.

(20) You can benefit from special terms on your initial order.

Unit 9 Offers

9.1 Introduction

An offer is a proposal of certain trade terms and an expression of willingness to make a contract or an agreement according to terms proposed. There are several issues in this unit: types of offers, letter content, notes, and sample letters.

9.2 Types of offers

In international trade, two parties conclude transactions depending on the stated terms and conditions. The one who states the terms and conditions in buying or selling a commodity, is the offering party; the condition he gives is the offer. When the buyer sends an offer, it is called a buying offer or bid; when the seller sends the offer, it is called a selling offer.

There are two kinds of offers in general; one is a firm offer, or offer of engagement; the other is a non-firm offer, or offer without engagement. A firm offer is sent when the seller or buyer is ready to sign the contract as soon as the terms are agreed upon. A firm offer should state the following points clearly: the name of the commodity, quality, specification, quantity, packing, price, delivery date and terms of payment including invoicing, transportation and insurance. A non-firm offer does not necessarily contain all the terms in a firm offer. It is not final; often with such words as "subject to prior sale" or "subject to our final confirmation".

9.3 Letter content

When making a firm offer, the party involved should:

1) Express thanks to the inquirer;

2) Give favorable comments on the products needed;
3) Supply all the information requested, including names of commodities, quality and specifications;
4) Give details of prices, discounts, terms of payment, packing, insurance, date of delivery, etc.;
5) State clearly the period for which the offer is valid. Use phrases such as "subject to your reply received by us (or before) ...", "subject to your acceptance within ... days" or "this offer is firm (open, valid, good) for ... days".
6) Express hope that the offer will be accepted and assure the customer of good service.

As price is composed of cost, charges, and profit, clear understanding of each part's constitution and its calculation is essential. In addition to correct calculation of various charges, it is very important for an exporter to set proper profit.

Production cost: the cost of producers used to produce certain product.

Processing cost: the cost used to process semi-product.

Purchasing cost: at what price that the exporter gets the commodity from home suppliers.

There are various expenses in import and export, such as packing fees, storage charges, domestic transportation fee, and fees for licenses of certificates, port charges, inspection fees, taxes, interests, operation costs, bank charges, freight, insurance premium, and commission.

A non-firm offer does not include the "point 5" of the firm offer, and sometimes might contain even fewer points. In a non-firm offer phrases, **such as** "without engagement, or obligation", "subject to prior sale" or "subject to our final confirmation" are often used.

Please note that unlike a quotation, a firm offer is a contractual obligation, and cannot be withdrawn by the seller within the time period stated in the offer. It is the buyer's option to accept, reject, or counter-offer during this time period. If the buyer accepts, then it is a contractual obligation. No reputable seller would risk his reputation by withdrawing his offer before the stated or agreed upon time.

9.4 Sample letters

(1)

Dear Sirs,

Re: Green Beans and Red Beans

We confirm receipt of your correspondence of August 28, asking us for firm offer for both Green Beans and Red Beans CFR Hamburg. We cabled back this morning, offering you 200 tons of Green Beans at US $... net per ton CFR Hamburg or any other European Main Ports for shipment during October/November, 2003. This offer is firm, subject to your reply received by us within one week. We wish to point out that this is the best price we can quote and that we are unable to entertain any counter-offer.

Regarding Red Beans, we should inform you that the few parcels we have at the present are under offer elsewhere. However, if you would make us an acceptable bid, there is a possibility that you could obtain these parcels.

No doubt you are aware that presently there has been a large demand for the above commodities and this growing demand can only result in increased prices. You can take advantage of this strengthening market by taking action on this offer immediately.

Sincerely,

(Signature)

(2)

28 June 2002

Dear Sirs,

We are very pleased to receive your inquiry of June 3 and confirm our cable this morning as follows, "eighty pounds per thirty-five yard piece FOB Liverpool subject to your reply reaching here within one week".

We must stress that this offer is firm for only one week because of the heavy demand for the limited supply of this velvet in stock.

The material is of the finest quality and we can assure you that as far as quality goes you have nothing to fear from the similar materials of other manufacturers either in this country or abroad. Certainly, you realize that the quoted price is very reasonable, however, weare anxious to do what we can to help establish with your new business and are prepared to allow you a special discount of 5% if your order exceeds $10,000.

If you decide to take advantage of our offer, kindly cable your acceptance.

Yours faithfully,

(Signature)

(**3**)

To whom it may concern,

We have seen your name and advertisements in various newspapers and periodicals in China, and we note that you are a leading importer of painting materials. Since 2001, our company has been the exporter of all sorts of painting materials, and we are confident that we can offer your company a great variety of high-quality painting materials at reasonable prices.

We enclose a copy of our latest sales catalog and price list. We hope you will be encouraged to lodge a trial order with us.

Sincerely yours,

(Signature)

9.5 Word study

(1) **Firm offer**: a price suggested for a service or a good that becomes legally fixed if accepted. Firm means not changing.

(2) **Bean**: a seed of any upright climbing plant, especially one that can be used as food. Beans are a good source of protein. In Britain and the USA people who are vegetarians (eat no meat) eat beans.

(3) **Port**: a place where ships can load and unload people or goods.

(4) **Point out**: to draw attention to a fact.

(5) **Advantage**: something that may help one to be successful or gain a favorable result.

(6) **Strengthen**: become or make strong or stronger.

(7) **Velvet**: a fine material made of silk and cotton, with a soft furry surface on one side only; velvet is thought of in connection with luxury.

(8) **Limited**: not very great in amount; not able to increase or improve.

(9) **In stock**: the total goods kept on hand by a merchant, commercial establishment, warehouse, or manufacturer.

(10) **Assure**: to tell firmly and with confidence, with the aim of removing doubt.

(11) **Reasonable**: not too much; fair; not expensive.

(12) **Anxious**: having a strong wish mixed with a feeling of anxiety.

(13) **Exceed**: to be greater than, to go beyond.

(14) **Take advantage of**: to make use of or profit from.

(15) **Periodical**: a publication that appears at fixed intervals.

(16) **Painting**: creating a picture with paints. *E. g.* He studied painting and sculpture for many years.

(17) **Variety**: things distinguished by some common characteristics or qualities. *E. g.* Sculpture is a form of art. What kinds of desserts are there? We have a wide variety of desserts.

(18) **Party**: a person or group of people concerned or taking part in an agreement, argument, or other activity, especially a legal matter.

Cultural notes:

(1) Lagos: The capital and largest city of Nigeria, in the southwest part of the country on the Gulf of Guinea. An old Yoruba town, it was the center of the nationalist movement before independence was achieved in 1960. Abuja was designated the new capital in 1982, but Lagos remains the economic and commercial center.

(2) Hamburg: A city of northern Germany on the Elbe River northeast of Bremen. Founded by Charlemagne as a defensive citadel in the early ninth century, the city quickly grew in commercial importance and in 1241 formed an alliance with Lvbeck that became the basis for the Hanseatic League. Today Hamburg is a major port and financial, industrial, and cultural center.

(3) Liverpool: Liverpool is still a big port, but it is much less important than it was in the 19th and early 20th centuries. Much of its industry has closed down, so there is fairly high unemployment in the area. In the 1960s, Liverpool became famous and very fashionable as the place where the BEATLES and several other bands started playing music. Football is very popular in Liverpool, and the city has two well-known teams, Liverpool and Everton. The stereotype of a person from Liverpool is someone who is working class, has socialist

political beliefs, and is good at telling jokes and making people laugh. People who come from Liverpool are called Liverpudlians, or informally Scousers. The Liverpool accent (way of pronouncing words) is very easy to recognize, and it is informally called a Scouse accent.

9.6 Useful sentences

(1) Due to high demand, there is little likelihood of goods remaining unsold. Our offer remains valid until October or until our stock is depleted.

(2) We have the pleasure of offering (quoting) you the following goods: ...

(3) We are interested in making you an offer on our hand-made carpets which are well received in the overseas market.

(4) For your consideration, we have put together an offer for our new products and hope you can take advantage of this opportunity.

(5) We are pleased to give you a quote for 1,500 dozen men's shirts per the sample you have sent. The price will be US $5 per piece CIF New York with prompt shipment.

(6) In compliance with your request, we are now offering you 2,000 dozen magnifiers at US $36 per dozen CIF San Francisco with September shipment.

(7) You will note from our fax that we are in a position to offer you 50 long tons of Tin Foil Sheets at an attractive price of £135 per long ton C&F Shanghai for delivery within one month after you place your order with us.

(8) The above prices are understood to be on CIF Karachi basis. A discount of 5% will be given if the quantity for each specification is more than 1,000 sets.

(9) Our quote is subject to a 5% commission.

(10) This firm offer is valid for 5 days.

(11) This special offer is not subject to our usual discount.

(12) We are happy to enclose our offer No. UE-1109 for your consideration. The price we quoted is on FOB Shanghai basis instead of on either FAS Shanghai or CIF Hong Kong basis. The offer will be valid until August 31, 2004.

(13) We are making you the following offer, subject to your acceptance reaching us no later than noon on December 23.

(14) We can offer you 30 metric tons of walnut meat, subject to your order reaching us before October 3rd Beijing time.

(15) The purchase payment is to be made by an irrevocable letter of credit, payable by draft in Pound Sterling in London.

(16) We would like to call your attention to our special offer (You should understand: not polite). Please note that this offer is good only if we receive your acceptance before the end of January. In view of the heavy demand for this line, we advise you to send your order as soon as possible.

(17) This morning you confirmed 50 tons of matchsticks as a firm offer, to be effective within a week.

(18) This is to confirm your cable for 20 tons of walnuts in a firm offer.

(19) Due to high demand, this offer is valid until January 10, while stock lasts. After the offer period, the goods will be sold.

(20) We sent you a cable this morning confirming our offer of 50 tons of matchsticks, subject to your reply reaching us within one week.

(21) We are confirming an offer of 20 tons of walnut-meat at Euro . . . per ton CIF European main ports for December shipment.

Unit 10 Counter Offers

10. 1 Introduction

A counter offer is made when a prospective buyer finds any terms or conditions in the offer unacceptable. A counter offer is a partial rejection of the original offer and also a counter proposal initiated by the buyer. The buyer may not agree to the price, packing, or shipment, and state his own terms instead. Such changes, no matter how slight they may appear to be, signify that the offer has to be re-negotiated. The original party making the offer has the right of acceptance or refusal. He may make an alternative counter offer of his own. This process can continue for many rounds until the offer is finalized or the business deal is called off. There are several important points in this unit as follows.

10. 2 Letter content

When a buyer rejects an offer, **he should**:

1) Thank the seller for his offer.
2) Express regret at his inability to accept the offer.
3) State the reasons for non-acceptance.
4) State that there may be other opportunities to do business together.

When a buyer makes a counter offer, the original seller now becomes the offeree. **The content includes**:

1) An expression of thanks for an offer or bid.
2) Regret being unable to accept what has been offered and state the reasons politely.
3) Make a counter offer if the circumstances are appropriate; put forward new terms and conditions.

4) State your hope for prompt reply and business success.

10.3 Notes

The writer must pay attention to the following **to avoid ambiguity or misunderstanding**:

1) State the terms explicitly.

2) Use proper words.

3) Express your intention accurately.

4) Write the letter sincerely and tactfully.

10.4 Sample letters

(1)

Dear Sirs,

<u>Groundnut Kernels FAQ19... Crop.</u>

We are in receipt of your letter of August 27 offering us 100 tons of the captioned goods at US $... per ton on the usual terms. In reply, we regret to inform you that our buyers in Rotterdam find your price much too high. Information indicates that some parcels from India have been sold at about 20% lower than yours.

We do not deny that the quality of Chinese kernels is slightly better, but the difference in price should not, nevertheless, be higher than ten percent. To expedite the trade, we counter offer as follows: subject to your acceptance received on or before September 20. 100 tons of groundnut kernels FAQ19... crop at US $... per ton CIF Rotterdam, with other terms as per your letter of August 27.

As the market is declining, we recommend your immediate acceptance.

Yours faithfully,

(Signature)

(2)

Dear Sirs,

We have now had the opportunity to examine the sample and patterns sent to us on August 2.

We agree with all prices quoted except the one for the microscope. These prices are not competitive enough for the market here, and we would therefore ask you to reduce them by 5 percent.

If you agree to the reduction in price, we are prepared to order up to US $50,000.

Yours faithfully,

(Signature)

(3)

Dear Sirs,

In reply to your counter offer of May 15, requesting 15% reduction in price, we regret to inform you that we cannot comply with your request.

The prices we offered were closely calculated in terms of the higher quality and market value of our products. We firmly believe, a fair comparison of quality between our products and similar goods from other sources will convince you that our quotations are quite fair.

We would appreciate it very much if you could reconsider our conditions and hope we can start building a mutually beneficial business relationship.

Yours faithfully,

(Signature)

10.5 Word study

(1) **Counter**: to act in order to oppose or defend oneself against stated terms.

(2) **Kernel**: the inner, usually edible seed of a nut or fruit stone.

(3) **FAQ**: fair average quality (also: Frequently Asked Questions).

(4) **Crop**: cultivated plants or agricultural produce, such as grain, vegetables, or fruit.

(5) **Caption**: words printed above or below a picture of newspaper article to say what it is about or give further information.

(6) **Indicate**: to show or make clear, especially by example.

(7) **Parcel**: a set of related things sold or offered as a unit.

(8) **Origin**: to have an established starting point. *E. g.* Indian origin.

(9) **Deny**: to declare untrue; refuse to accept as a fact.

(10) **Slightly**: small in degree which is not considerable, noticeable, or serious.

(11) **Recommend**: to advice or suggest as a correct or suitable course of action.

(12) **Pattern**: a model considered worthy of imitation. *E. g.* The American constitution has provided a pattern for many republics.

(13) **Reduce**: cut down on; make a reduction in. *E. g.* Reduce your daily fat intake; The employer wants to reduce health benefits.

(14) **Competitive**: involving competition or competitiveness. *E. g.* competitive games; to improve one's competitive position.

(15) **Calculate**: make a mathematical calculation or computation.

(16) **Comparison**: examining similarities or differences.

(17) **Convince**: get someone to agree, understand, or realize the truth or validity of something. *E. g.* He had finally convinced several customers of the advantages of his product.

(18) **Mutually**: in a mutual or shared manner. *E. g.* The agreement was mutually satisfactory; the goals of the negotiators were not mutually exclusive.

Cultural notes:

Rotterdam: Rotterdam is a city in the southwest Netherlands on the Rhine-Meuse delta south-southeast of The Hague. Chartered in 1328, it was a major commercial power during the 16th and 17th centuries and is today a thriving port accessible via canal to ocean-going vessels. The city was heavily bombed during World War II.

10. 6 Useful sentences

(1) We would like to counter offer as follows:...

(2) Our counter offer is well founded.

(3) Due to a shortage of stock, we regret that we are unable to accept your offer.

(4) We regret that you have turned down our counter offer.

(5) If you accept our counter offer, we will inform our end-users to buy from you.

(6) This is our lowest price; we cannot make any further reductions.

(7) Your quotation is on the high (low) side.

(8) The price you counter offered is in (out of) line with the prevailing market.

(9) Please make us a reasonable counter offer.

(10) The prices you quoted are much higher than those of other suppliers.

(11) We regret to say that your price for iron nails is out of line with the market here.

(12) The market is not as active this year as it was last year. If you can reduce your limit by 3%, there is a possibility we can do business with you.

(13) Thank you for your quotation for the supply of Bitter Apricot Kernels. However, it was necessary to place our order elsewhere because your prices are too high for this market.

(14) Regretfully, we are unable to accept your price; it is too high and out of line with current market levels.

(15) If you can reduce your price by 4%, we are ready to place an order with you for 500 sets "Huanan" Brand Sewing Machines.

(16) We cannot possibly conduct business unless you reduce your price by 2 percent.

(17) I sincerely hope we can find some common ground to this problem. I would like to hear your opinion.

(18) We have received offers much lower than yours. If you can reduce your price by 4%, we will have the opportunity to conduct business.

(19) As the market is declining, we cannot accept your offer unless your price goes down.

(20) In order to finalize our business agreement, we will lower our price a little, but cannot reduce it to the extent you indicated.

Unit 11 Orders

11.1 Introduction

Letters dealing with orders for merchandise form the bulk of business letter writing activity. As a result, serious thinking and care should be exercised when drafting these letters. A little carelessness may result in loss of the customer's good-will. Therefore order letters should be exact, cordial, and tactful. They should be detailed and complete so that the readers can interpret it exactly as the writer wishes. Any error or incompleteness may mean further correspondence, shipping delays, complicated billing, repacking, or loss of business. This unit discusses several points: the letter content; the way to deal with a first order; the notes to write; and sample letters.

11.2 Letter content

An order may result from an offer or an inquiry with subsequent quotations. Orders may be requested by a letter, memorandum, by telephone or email, or orally at a meeting. Usually there is no correspondence at all. Instead, buyers use printed order forms and sellers use printed acknowledgments. The order includes **the following items**:

1) Full details including description, quantities, prices, and state product numbers, if any.

2) State type of packing, port of destination, and time of shipment.

3) Confirm the terms of payment as agreed upon in preliminary negotiations.

Sometimes, buyers will seek to protect themselves by making their order subject to certain penalties should the contracted terms not be fulfilled. A penalty is a punishment established by law or authority for a crime or an offense.

11.3 Dealing with the first order

If the order comes from **a new customer**, you should always **acknowledge it by a letter**.

1) You should express pleasure in receiving the order.
2) Use positive comments in the letter about the goods ordered to indicate the buyer has made a right decision.
3) Promise you will give prompt and careful attention.
4) Draw attention to other products you are offering to increase more business opportunities.
5) End the letter by expressing hope to receive more orders.

Sometimes a seller cannot accept the buyer's order because the goods ordered are not available or the price and specifications have changed. You can write a rejection letter, but at the same time, keep goodwill for future business. You can suggest some other goods as substitutes, or make counter-offers. You can also persuade the buyer to accept something new.

11.4 Notes

After mutual negotiation, a transaction may finally be completed. A negotiation generally includes four steps: inquiry, offer, counter offer, and acceptance. An order is a result of negotiations, placed by a buyer, which is a demand to buy an exact amount of goods.

In order messages, the main topic of the first paragraph is reserving or ordering something. The explanatory paragraphs give whatever details the order requires—quantity, color, style, size, specification, price, payment, location, shipment data, place—plus any specific instructions the reader might need.

The last paragraph invites prompt shipment and processing dates, if desired. An order letter needs not be preceded by an inquiry or offer. Information received from catalogue and advertisements assist customers in placing an order that can result in a sale. Hence it has great importance. Proper care should be taken in drafting of the order to ensure efficient handling and to eliminate any doubts that could result in loss of time and possabilaty of market changes.

After receiving an order, the seller may immediately confirm the acceptance if he can accept all the terms and conditions stipulated in it. An acceptance or a confirmation is an unreserved agreement between the buyers and the sellers.

In the field of international trade, a trading company will produce a sales confirmation or sales contract, abbreviated as S/C, in duplicate after conclusion of a deal. The company signs the S/C in duplicate and then sends them to the buyer to be counter-signed. The original S/C should be returned to be kept on file. A S/C signed by both buyer and seller is a binding contract for both parties. The buyer and the supplier must fulfill their obligation in compliance with the terms of the contract.

According to commercial law, the buyers' order is an offer to buy and that arrangement is not legally binding until the seller has accepted the offer. Once the offer is accepted, both parties are legally bound to honor their agreement.

When a binding agreement is made, the buyer is required by law to carry out three obligations: to accept the goods supplied, provided they comply with the terms of the order; to pay for the goods according to the terms agreed upon; and to check the goods as soon as possible. If the buyer does not give prompt notice of any mistakes to the seller, it will be taken as acceptance of the goods. The seller also has some obligations such as: deliver goods exactly as ordered, and at the agreed time; guarantee that the products supplied are free from faults that the buyer may have not been aware of at the time of purchase.

If the wrong goods are delivered, the buyer has the right to take action. The buyer can ask for a reduction in price, replacement of the goods, cancellation of the order, or even make a claim against the seller for the losses he/she has sustained.

11.5 Sample letters

(1) An order letter

Dear Sirs,

Re: Canned Mushrooms

We are pleased by your prompt reply to our inquiry of December 20, 2008 and wish to place an order of canned mushrooms from you. We are enclosing our purchase order of canned mushrooms for your action.

We will open an irrevocable L/C in your favor through the First National City Bank, New York, to cover the total CIF value of this order. We appreciate your arranging to ship upon receipt of the L/C the first four items by the first available vessel sailing to New York.

Please send one sample tin of the six types of products we have ordered by air, and express and confirm your acceptance of our order by return mail.

Yours sincerely,

(Signature)

(2) Acknowledgment of an order

July 19, 2002

Dear Sirs,

"Five Rams" Brand White Cement

As a result of our recent exchange of telegrams, we confirm our order of 1,500 tons of the captioned goods from your company on the following terms and conditions:

Price: at $315 per ton CFR Genoa, net shipping weight.

Packing: in 6-ply Kraft-paper bags of about 110 lbs net each.

Quality: against the seller's own guarantee that the goods are fully up to the China Export standard.

Shipment: one or two lots to be shipped from Huangpu to Genoa during March 2002 preferably by direct steamer.

Payment: by a confirmed and irrevocable L/C in your favor, payable by draft at sight.

We are pleased to have conducted this first business with your corporation and look forward to the further expansion of trade to our mutual benefit.

Yours faithfully,

(Signature)

(3) Acceptance of an Order

Dear Sirs,

We thank you for your fax of November 5th confirming your order of 120 dozen MouTai Chiew.

Alcohol Content: 55% –57%.

Capacity: 500 grams per bottle.

Price: HK $... per dozen CIF Antwerp.

Shipment: November 2006.

Although the current market price is a little bit higher, we accept the order on the same terms as before to encourage future business. As requested in your previous letter, we enclose our Sales Confirmation in triplicate. Please send back one fully signed copy.

Be assured that your order will receive our full attention.

Yours faithfully,

(Signature)

11.6 Word study

(1) **Mushroom**: any of various fleshy fungi of the subdivision Basidiomycete consisting of a cap at the end of a stem arising from an underground mycelium.

(2) **Purchase**: the acquisition of something for payment. They closed the purchase with a handshake.

(3) **Letter of credit (L/C)**: a document issued by a bank that guarantees the payment of a customer's draft; substitutes the bank's credit for the customer's credit.

(4) **Vessel**: a craft designed for water transportation.

(5) **Cement**: a building material made by grinding calcined limestone and clay to a fine powder, which can be mixed with water and poured to set as a solid mass or used as an ingredient in making mortar or concrete.

(6) **Kraft**: a tough, usually brown paper made from wood pulp treated with a solution of sodium sulfate, used chiefly for bags and wrapping paper.

(7) **Guarantee**: a promise or an assurance, especially one given in writing that attests to the quality or durability of a product or service.

(8) **Steamer**: a vehicle, a machine, or an engine driven by steam.

(9) **Mutual**: possessed in common.

(10) **Ram**: an adult male sheep.

(11) **Brand**: the goods of a particular company or producer. *E. g.* The brand name of this soap is "flower".

(12) **Recent**: having happened or come into existence only a short time ago.

(13) **Ply**: a measure of the thickness.

(14) **Against**: Indicates opposition to or conflict with somebody or something either physically or intellectually, in competition with, in contact with by leaning.

(15) **Standard**: a level or degree of quality that is considered proper or acceptable.

(16) **Preferably**: specifies more exactly what is required or desired. *E. g.* Plan to arrive early, preferably before the rush hour.

(17) **CFR**: formerly known as C&F, stands for Cost and Freight (named port of destination). On a CFR contract, the seller arranges the shipment of the goods and pays the freight to the named port of destination. The buyer bears the risk of loss or damage to the goods once they are loaded on board of the ship at the named port of shipment. As for insurance, it is entirely the buyer's responsibility, including payment of premiums.

(18) **Acceptance**: the mental attitude that something is believable and should be accepted as true. *E. g.* He gave a cceptance to the gossip; Acceptance of Newtonian mechanics was unquestioned for 200 years.

(19) **Dozen**: denoting a quantity consisting of 12 items or units.

(20) **Alcohol**: a liquor or brew containing alcohol as the active agent.

(21) **Capacity**: the amount that can be contained. *E. g.* The gas tank has a capacity of 12 gallons.

(22) **Antwerp**: a port in northern Belgium on the Scheldt River.

(23) **Triplicate**: one of three copies; any of three things that correspond to one another exactly.

(24) **Cancel**: give up a planned activity or event; state or decide that something will not happen.

(25) **Punctual**: not late or doing something at the time promised.

11.7 Useful sentences

(1) We send you the following trial order based on your estimate of March 10.

(2) We want you to deliver products that exactly match the sample. Any substitutions will not be accepted.

(3) As we happily conclude this initial transaction with you, we sincerely hope that it will pave the way for mutually beneficial business in the future.

(4) It is our hope that this order is the first step to establish a long and pleasant business relationship between us.

(5) If our first order is satisfactorily executed, we will place additional orders with you.

(6) We place our order, subject to your guarantee that the material you supply is absolutely waterproof.

(7) We are giving your order our immediate attention, and you can depend on us to deliver well within your time limit.

(8) Your order has been placed and will be handled with great care. Please open the relevant L/C, which must reach us one month before the date of shipment.

(9) We have enclosed our order, but must point out that the falling market here will leave us little or no margin of profit.

(10) We must ask you for a better price for future orders. It is regrettable to see an order dropped because no agreement on price can be reached; however, we would like to recommend another product at a lower price for your consideration.

(11) As a trial order, we are delighted to send you a small shipment for 80 men's shirts S/500.

(12) Because our order is urgently needed, we find it necessary to stress the importance of making punctual shipment; any delay in shipment would result in our withdrawal of this order.

(13) When the purchase is made and the price confirmed, I will let you know when they will be invoiced.

(14) We are able to expedite your full order with the exception of the pepper parcel, which has been sold.

(15) Your samples of ... received favorable reaction from our customers, and we are pleased to enclose our order for ...

(16) We are pleased to enclose a repeat order, as follows: ...

(17) We are enclosing our Confirmation of Purchase in duplicate; please sign and return one copy for our reference.

(18) Unfortunately, we cannot accept new orders due to ...

(19) Due to the fact that some items in your order are beyond our business scope, we can only accept part of your order. We hope this will not cause you any inconvenience.

(20) Much to our regret, we presently cannot accept your order due to a large volume of previous commitments.

(21) We find both the price and quality of your products satisfactory, and are pleased to give you an order for the following items with the understanding that

they will be supplied from current stock at the prices quoted.

(22) Please supply 6 dozen each of the product in red, yellow, green, blue and brown.

(23) If you can accept US $2. 15 per set, send us a pro-forma invoice and we will open a letter of credit for 1, 200 sets. The quality of the merchandise must match that of your sample.

(24) In view of your urgent need for the goods, and taking into consideration the good relationship between our companies, we can only fulfill your order by putting off another customer.

(25) If you fail to deliver the goods within the specified time, we have no alternative but to cancel the order.

(26) Although your price is below our levels, we will make an exception and accept your order with the intent of establishing future business dealings with you.

(27) The exceptional demand for this market line makes it impossible to promise delivery of any further orders before October.

(28) Due to our current heavy volume of commitments, we are not in a position to accept your order at the present time.

(29) We confirm and thank you for your kind order dated May 10 for 1, 000 "Lenovo" brand computers.

(30) We place this trial order on the clear understanding that delivery to our warehouse in Zhuhai has to take place before June 9.

Unit 12 Complaints

12. 1 Introduction

In doing business, it is necessary to abide by contracts in good faith. If one party fails to carry out the terms of the contract, the other will file a complaint or claim for losses that result from the breach of contract. Sometimes when the loss is not serious, the party that suffers from the loss may not lodge a claim for compensation. Instead, he writes a complaint letter to call the other party's attention to this matter, to prevent it from happening again. There are several topics discussed in this unit: types of complaints; letter content; notes to write; dealing with a complaint and sample letters.

12. 2 Types of complaints

In general, there are two kinds of complaints: a genuine complaint, which is the usual complaint made by the buyers; and a complaint, which is used as an excuse to get out of the contract.

The genuine complaint may arise from some legitimate conditions. For example, the wrong goods may have been sent; or the quality of the goods received is not satisfactory when compared with what was ordered; or the goods may have been delivered damaged, late; or the price charged might be higher than what they agreed upon.

Sometimes a buyer files a complaint as an excuse to get out of the contract. This can happen because either he no longer wants the goods or because he has found cheaper goods elsewhere. If buyer has made a complaint, the matter should be investigated in details, and these details should be laid before the party charged.

12.3 Letter content

In writing letters of complaint, the following points are induded:

1) Regret for the need to complain.
2) Statement of the date of the contract, delivery terms, and the products purchased.
3) Reference to the inconvenience or loss incurred.
4) Suggest a solution.

12.4 Notes

Admittedly, making complaints is not a pleasant business and needs to be well planned and documented. The followings are some guidelines to help you ensure that the complaint receives a proper adjustment. When you have to make a complaint, you should directly state what is wrong, identify the specific situation, and describe the circumstances in a clear and organized way. You should present enough facts to allow a decision, name specific actions that can correct the problem, and in polite yet strong terms. Mention what the consequences will be if you do not get a satisfactory reply. Lastly, end the letter on a positive note—be friendly but firm.

12.5 Dealing with a complaint

Imagine you have received a complaint, how do you deal with it? **When answering complaints, you must:**

1) Politely mention receiving the letter of complaint.
2) If the complaint is legitimate, admit the mistake, and offer a reasonable solution. If the complaint is not legitimate, politely state the reasons why you cannot accept the complaint or claim.
3) If the complaint or claim is justified, promise not to make the same mistake in future transactions. If the complaint is not justified, express your appreciation to the party for his efforts to make things clear.
4) If you have received a complaint but you cannot deal with it immediately, you should send a note at once. Express your regret; explain the reasons

why you cannot address the problem right away. Let them know that you will investigate the complaint fully and will send the result as soon as possible.

5) You should treat each complaint seriously and make thorough investigation.

Replies to complaints should always be courteous. Even if the complaint is unfounded, the seller should not say so until they have reliable grounds on which to repudiate the complaint. It is not necessary for the sellers to go into a long story of how the mistake was made, a short explanation is enough.

12.6 Sample letters

(1) Complaint for non-conformity of quality

Dear Sirs,

After carefully examining the velvet shipped on the S. S. East Wind, we can only express disappointment at the quality of the shipment. The consignment certainly does not match the samples you sent us before we placed our order. Some of the pieces are in such a poor condition that we cannot help but feel there must have been a mistake in packing the consignment.

The materials are not suited to the needs of our customers and we have no choice but to ask you to take them back and replace them with the quality material as specified in the order. If this is not possible, we are afraid we will have to terminate our contract.

We trust that you will look into this matter and send us a prompt reply.

Yours truly,

(Signature)

(2) Complaint of delays in delivery

Gentlemen:

Re: 500 Dozen Cotton Bath Towels

We regret we have to complain about late delivery of the captioned goods we ordered on September 14. Although you guaranteed delivery in November, we did not receive the goods until the end of this month. We placed the order with you based on this guarantee.

Unfortunately, there have been similar delivery problems on several occasions in the past, and in recent months it has occurred more often. We regret to say that under these conditions the business between us cannot be continued.

We feel it is necessary to make our position on this matter clearly known. If we cannot rely on our suppliers guaranteed time of delivery, it is impossible for us to give our customers a satisfactory explanation. With this understanding, we expect that you will deliver our orders on time from this point forward.

Yours truly,
(Signature)

(3) Complaint about merchandise that does not match the samples

Dear Sirs,

Thank you for shipping our order No. WDY-A2. However, we are sorry to inform you that the overcoat order we have received is not the same high quality as the samples we received on June 9. We cannot accept this delivery and must ask you to replace the entire collection.

We expect you to deal with this problem without delay.

We are terribly sorry to inform you that the overcoat order (our order No. WDY – A2) we received is not up to the quality of the samples which we received on June 9.

Comparing the overcoats we have with the samples, we were surprised to find that the models are not the same high quality. We think something is wrong and we cannot accept this delivery. We must ask for replacement of this entire collection.

We expect you to deal with this problem without delay.

Yours faithfully,
(Signature)

12.7 Word study

(1) **Complaint**: a statement of annoyance, dissatisfaction about something or against somebody.

(2) **Conformity**: agreement with established rules, customs.

(3) **Consign**: to send something to a person or place for sale. *E. g.* The goods are

consigned to you by railway; Consignment means a quantity of goods consigned together.

(4) **Prompt**: done quickly, at once, at the right time.

(5) **Delivery**: the act of taking or giving something to someone.

(6) **Guarantee**: a formal declaration that something will be done, especially a written agreement by the maker of an article to repair or replace it if it is found to be imperfect within a given period of time.

(7) **Rely on**: to trust that something will happen or someone will do something; have confidence in.

(8) **Overcoat**: a heavy coat worn over clothes in winter.

(9) **Consequence**: something that happens because of an action or set of conditions; the result.

12.8 Useful sentences

(1) The goods under our order No. 5501 should have reached us a week ago.

(2) Six cases of the shipment were badly damaged when delivered on October 7th.

(3) After checking the goods against your invoice, we discovered a considerable shortage in the number received.

(4) The buyers have filed a claim on the shipment for RMB 2, 000.

(5) We claim US $3, 400 for a short shipment of the 60 tons of peanuts delivered by the S. S. Dongfeng.

(6) We request to extend the time limit for filing claims until the middle of March on the above captioned shipment.

(7) Our check for US $3, 700 was airmailed to you today in settlement of your claim for short weight of 600 lbs.

(8) Your claim needs to be supported by sufficient evidence.

(9) We have received many complaints from our customers about the watches from our order No. 220.

(10) After investigation, we find that the quality of the goods is not in compliance with the contract stipulations.

(11) I am writing to complain about the poor quality of the product we bought from your enterprise last month, and about the impolite behavior of your new sales representative.

(12) We are returning the poor quality goods to your company for a replacement.

(13) Thank you for your letter in response to our complaint. However, we firmly believe that our company does not have any responsibility for this damage and suggest that you should go to court to settle this disagreement.

(14) We are seriously disappointed to find out that the quality of the underwear for young women you sent us does not match the samples you submitted in May.

(15) In my opinion, the only way to solve the problem is to issue us a refund—the goods are not what we ordered.

(16) Considering these conditions, you should give us a 10 zx reduction in price; or you can take back your goods.

(17) We demand a formal investigation of our complaint. Please be considerate and do not damage your reputation any further.

(18) You have 24 hours to admit your fault; otherwise we will turn the entire matter to our lawyer.

(19) If you cannot solve this outrageous situation within two days, I will send my complaint directly to your top manager.

(20) When I checked the boxes, I found that they did not contain the ordered items. Instead, it contained totally different equipment.

Unit 13 Claims

13. 1 Introduction

In international business, claims do not happen in every transaction but occur often. Most claims occur because a seller's breach of contract, a buyer's breach of contract, or unclear stipulations in contracts. Claims are usually filed by buyers for loss caused by short delivery, inferior quality, non-delivery, or delay in delivery, damage of goods, or shortage of quantity and improper packing. However, sellers can also raise claims against buyers for non-establishment of L/C. Claims should be supported by recognizable evidence or reports. Usually an official commodity inspection certificate, together with other appropriate evidence will suffice. Claims are usually raised for serious loss. When one party receives a claim, he has three choices: settle the claim; make some adjustment to the claim; or reject the claim. This unit addresses the following topics: rules for filing a claim, how to deal with a claim, notes, and sample letters.

13. 2 Rules for filing a claim

When writing a claim letter, first state the problem with as much information as possible; then tell the reader how inconvenient it has been for you and tell them what you want to be done. After investigation, if the claim is found reasonable, it must be settled. Letters of settlement should be written with restraint and tact in order not to jeopardize further business relationships. **When making a direct claim, observe the following points:**

1) Make clear what your claim is.
2) Don't let your anger show in your writing and avoid sarcasm.
3) Give the facts—calmly, specifically, and thoroughly.

4) Request the action you expect: a replacement, repair, refund, or compensation.

5) Make sure that your letter will not cause resentment or be offensive. The tone and wording of your letter must be clearly understood.

13.3 Dealing with a claim

When dealing with a claim, keep the following points in mind:

1) Begin your communication pleasantly by stating the details of the adjustment. Avoid any grudging or disappointing tone.

2) Explain fully, honestly and reassuringly any favorable facts. Include a goodwill-building sentence saying that you welcome the customer's comments as a way to make future improvements. State briefly the reason for the mishap. Be quick to admit the mistake if the product or the company's service was at fault.

3) Ask for any necessary cooperation from the customer.

4) Close your correspondence pleasantly with a look toward the future. Do not repeatedly rehash or apologize for the disappointing episode. Close your letter with assurance that the situation will be resolved and express your desire for future business.

13.4 Sample letters

(1) **Claim for damages**

Dear Sirs,

Re: Claim on Tea Sets under S/C No. 898

The 250 cases of Tea Sets under the above S/C No. 898 arrived in Amsterdam on March 16 by the S. S. Peace. Much to our regret, about 20% of the packages was seriously damaged with their contents shattered to pieces and outer bands broken.

Qualified surveyors were immediately invited to investigate the case, and their findings show that this was due to careless packing. A detailed survey report will be dispatched to you, subsequent to further study of individual cases.

In accordance with the stipulations of the above S/C, the Tea Sets should have been packed in strong wooden cases suitable for long distance ocean voyages. Under these circumstances, we are obliged to hold you responsible for the damage and are making a claim for compensation for the loss we incurred.

Meanwhile, our buyers are urging us to settle the case immediately. You are therefore requested to inform us what you decide to do regarding our loss.

We await your earliest reply.

Yours faithfully,

(Signature)

Jan Sloot Trading Company

Jan Sloot

(2) **Claims for poor packing**

Dear Sirs,

Re: "National" Brand Transistor Radio Sets under order No. 1596

We regret to inform you that the "National" Brand Transistor Radio sets sent to cover our order No. 1596, shipped by S. S. Victories, arrived in such an unsatisfactory condition that we must file a claim against you. Upon careful examination, it was found that nearly 15% of the packages had been broken, obviously attributed to improper packing. Our only recourse was to have them repacked before delivery to our customers, which inevitably resulted in extra expenses in the amount of $800. We expect to be reimbursed by you for this additional expense.

We also would like to take this opportunity to suggest that special care be taken in your future deliveries. Prospective customers are apt to misjudge the quality of your goods because of the faulty packing.

Yours truly,

(Signature)

(3) Settlement of a claim

China National Chemical Fertilizer
Import & Export Corporation
P. O. Box No. 65
Shanghai
People's Republic of China
March 19th
The Universal Trading Company
32 Tower Street
Liverpool
England

Dear Sirs,

Re: Your claim on Chemical Fertilizer

With reference to your letter of March 9, which indicates a claim has been lodged for a short delivery of 1, 500 pounds of chemical fertilizer, we wish to express our deepest regret over the unfortunate incident. You must have had difficulties meeting the orders of your clients.

After a review by our staff at the warehouse in Liverpool, it was found that some 100 bags had not been packed in 5-ply strong paper bags as stipulated in the contract resulting in breakage during transit. This was due entirely to the negligence of the warehouse managers, for which we, the exporters, offer our apologies.

In view of our long-standing business relations with you, we will make payment by check for $450 (the amount of your claim), into your account with the Bank of China upon receipt of your acceptance.

We hope this matter will not affect our good relationship with your company and will not stand in the way of future business.

Yours faithfully,
(Signature)
China National Chemical Fertilizer Import & Export Corporation,
Hong. Li
Manager

(4) **Claim rejected**

Dear Sir or Madam,

M. V. "East Wind" 2,000 tons of Maize

We have received your letter of September 16, filing a claim with us for the loss and damage to the captioned goods.

Last month, on her voyage from Kobe to Guangzhou, the M. V. "East Wind" encountered heavy weather incessantly with torrential rains. The log showed that the hold ventilators had to be closed for some length of time to guard against ingress of fresh water into the hold. It is precisely because of this protective measure that sweat formed in the hold, which resulted in the maize being dampened. This is an event beyond our control and on the strength of the provision of the Bill of Lading and therefore we cannot hold ourselves responsible for the loss.

We trust that you will fully understand our position.

Yours truly,

(Signature)

13.5 Word study

(1) **Claim**: a demand or request for reparation to which you have a right to.

(2) **Damage**: the harm or loss that results from the process of spoiling the condition or quality of something.

(3) **Import**: something brought into a country from another country.

(4) **Export**: to send goods out of a country for sale in another country.

(5) **Corporation**: a group of people who are permitted by law to act as a single unit, especially for the purpose of business, with rights and duties separated from those of its members.

(6) **Set**: a group of connected things. *E. g.* a 21-piece tea set (cups, plates, and teapot); a chess set (all the pieces needed to play the game).

(7) **Case**: a case is a large box or container, in which goods can be stored, moved, or for holding and protecting something.

(8) **Package**: a number of things packed together; a parcel.

(9) **Seriously**: not easy to deal with; causing worry and needing attention; not a slight problem.

(10) **Shatter**: to cause to break or burst suddenly into pieces, as with a violent

blow.

(11) **Surveyor**: a person whose job is to professionally examine the condition of something.

(12) **Investigate**: to make a detailed inquiry or systematic examination to determine a conclusive statement.

(13) **Stipulation**: something required, especially a term or condition in an agreement.

(14) **Pack**: to put something into a case or box to transport it.

(15) **Voyage**: a journey by sea to a foreign or distant land.

(16) **Be obliged to**: a requirement for someone to do something.

(17) **Compensate**: to provide a suitable payment for a loss or damage. *E. g.* The union is seeking compensation for two factory workers who were dismissed yesterday.

(18) **Poor packing**: not the usual standard; low in quality.

(19) **Transistor**: a small electrical apparatus, especially found in a small radio that controls the flow of an electrical current.

(20) **Cover**: to deal with, take into account.

(21) **Unsatisfactory**: not good enough to be pleasing, or not up to standards set for a particular purpose.

(22) **Improper**: not suitable, not correct, not in accordance with the rules.

(23) **Recourse**: the action of doing something as a means of help.

(24) **Prospect**: a person who may buy a company's products or service.

(25) **Apt to**: is inclined to; tend to. *E. g.* He is apt to lose his temper.

(26) **Reject**: refuse to accept or consider.

(27) **M. V.** : the short form of motor vessel; ship, large boat.

(28) **Maize**: sweet corn; Indian corn; a type of tall plant grown in America and Australia; its yellow seeds can be used as food for people and animals.

(29) **Encounter**: to meet or have to deal with; be faced with.

(30) **Incessantly**: continuous over a long period of time; never stopping.

(31) **Torrential**: a violently rushing stream especially of water.

(32) **Log**: an official written record of a journey, especially in a ship or a plane.

(33) **Hold**: the part of a ship below deck where goods are stored.

(34) **Ventilator**: an apparatus to allow or cause fresh air to enter and move around inside a room, thus driving out bad air, smoke, or gas.

(35) **Ingress**: the act of entering or the right to enter.
(36) **Protective**: to guard property against possible loss or damage.
(37) **Sweat**: to show liquid on the surface, coming from inside.
(38) **On the strength of**: because of; persuaded or influenced by.
(39) **Bill of lading**: an official document stating that goods to be shipped have been received and gives the conditions under which they arrived.

13.6 Useful sentences

(1) We have received the 15 cases of chinaware you sent us, but regret to say that upon examination, six of them were in a badly damaged condition. This apparently is due to faulty packing.
(2) We examined them one by one, and found that each of them was leaking.
(3) We regret to inform you that one of the cases of your consignment arrived in a badly damaged condition. It looks as if the case was not strong enough to stand the voyage. We have examined the contents and found that half of the goods are unusable.
(4) Your shipment of our order has been found short in weight. We regret that we must lodge a claim amounting to £2,000 (this amount includes a survey fee).
(5) Carton 20 was found to be 60 pieces short. The carton was in good shape and did not appear to have been tampered with; we can only surmise that it must have been short shipped.
(6) The goods you sent do not meet our satisfaction; the quality is very poor and therefore unsuitable for the demands of this market.
(7) We appreciate your prompt attention to correcting these errors.
(8) The quality of the shipment for our order No. T52 does not conform to the sample. Therefore we must file a claim against you for the amount of £3,200.
(9) The goods that were delivered are not up to the standard of your samples. The pattern is uneven in some places and the color quality varies.
(10) The goods arrived two weeks late without any explanation.
(11) We must insist upon greater punctuality regarding our deliveries. Otherwise, we will be forced to place our orders with others who can and will deliver at the predetermined time.
(12) None of the items in this case is of any use to us; pending your reply, we will

hold them for your disposal.

(13) In spite of our repeated requests, we regret that your refusal to establish L/C for the pending contract results in a breach of contract.

(14) You may return the wrong order by the next available vessel for our company; however, we prefer you to dispose of them in your market. We will compensate you with a 10% commission.

(15) We regret that faulty sets were sent to you and will send you a replacement of 200 sets next week. We hope you will be pleased with the new lot.

(16) It would not be fair to impose the total loss on us, as the liability rests with both parties. We are ready to pay only 50% of the loss.

(17) With mutual cooperation, this case has been settled amicably and we will remit the amount of US $3, 100 to compensate the loss.

(18) We are prepared to send you reasonable compensation for your claim, but not the amount you have requested. We don't understand why the loss amount should be twice the actual value of the goods. Please reconsider this matter and get back to us.

(19) We are open to compromise, but the reparation should not exceed US $310; otherwise, this case will be submitted to arbitration.

(20) We thank you for calling our attention to this error. We have taken necessary precautions to prevent a reoccurrence of similar mistakes in the future.

(21) Please note that the goods were dispatched in perfect condition and we are not responsible for damage in transit unless as we had recommended, wooden cases were used.

(22) This is an insurance matter and we recommend that you refer the claim to the insurance company at your end.

(23) The document provided to support your claim is insufficient; therefore we cannot consider the claim for compensation.

(24) The pilferage may have happened on the voyage because strict inspection of the goods was done before packing, and the carrier apparently received them in good order.

(25) Color deviation that exists between the products and the sample is normal and permissible. Therefore the compensation claim is not viable.

(26) Your claim for indemnity for the loss you sustained should, in our opinion, be referred to the shipping company as the liability rests with them.

(27) We must remind you of the sale conditions, which state that all goods are shipped at the risk of the buyer and that we will not be responsible for anything that happens to the goods after they leave Tokyo.

(28) Claims must be submitted within 30 days after the arrival of the goods at their destination or they will not be considered.

(29) Please accept our sincere apologies for the inconvenience that the delay in processing the claim of January 24 has caused you.

(30) Thank you for your claim pointing that the wrong goods have been sent. We will refund you as soon as possible and assure you that this kind of behavior will never happen again to you, our valued customer.

Unit 14 Insurance

14.1 Introduction

Shipment insurance was originally applied only to losses at sea, where risks were always greater. Nowadays in order to protect the goods, the buyer or seller applies to an insurance company for insurance covering all the goods in transit. There are various kinds of risks that can be covered under an insurance policy. The transportation insurance types include ocean marine transportation insurance, overland transportation insurance, air transportation insurance, and parcel post insurance. Ocean marine transportation insurance is widely used in international trade businesses.

People get insurance because they want someone to compensate them for the losses or damages they have suffered. Thus insurance is a contract of indemnity, which compensates the insured for either the full amount of the loss or a specified percentage of the amount. There are several topics in this unit: some concepts about insurance, notes to write, and sample letters.

14.2 Notes

The contract between the insurer and insured is called insurance policy. The insurer agrees to accept the risk and compensate the insured a stated sum or a portion of a loss. This portion has to be within the scope of risk coverage. The insured has the duty to pay the insurer insurance premium, which is quoted as a percentage of the sum insured. The insurance policy is a legal document setting out the exact terms and conditions of an insurance transaction. The name of the insured, the name of the commodity insured, the amount insured, the name of the carrying vessel covered, the precise risks covered, the period of coverage and any exceptions should be included.

There are several concepts related to insurance. They are risks, losses, and expenses. According to the loss or damage caused by risks included in different coverage and the expenses involved, the insurance company is responsible for indemnifying the insured goods. Risks refer to loss and coverage, which are closely related to each other. Marine Risks can be classified into two categories, perils at the sea and extraneous risks. Natural calamities and accidents usually cause the risks at the sea. It should be noted that Marine Risks do not include all the risks at sea. For instance, fresh water damage is not included in Marine Risks. Extraneous risks are caused by extraneous reasons, beyond the coverage of the Marine Risks, consisting of General Extraneous Risks and Special Extraneous Risks.

Transportation insurance not only insures the losses caused by risks but also the losses of expenses. Marine losses are the damages or losses of the insured goods incurred by perils of the sea. According to the extent of the damage, losses in marine insurance fall into two types. Total Loss includes actual total loss and constructive total loss, and Partial Loss includes general average and particular average.

Legal and labor expenses arise from measures properly taken by the insured, the employee, and the assignee for minimizing or avoiding losses caused by the risks covered in the insurance policy. The insurer is held responsible to compensate such expenses. Salvage charges are expenses resulting from measures properly taken by a third party other than the insured, the employee, and the assignee.

An insurance claims should be submitted to the insurance company or its agent as promptly as possible. In order to substantiate an average claim on cargo, the following documents must be presented; insurance policy or certificate, bill of lading, original invoice, survey report, formal protest, and statement of claim.

14.3 Sample letters

(1)

Dear Sirs,

In response to your letter dated September 20, in regard to insurance, we would like to inform you of the following:

ALL RISKS: Generally we cover insurance against WPA and War Risk in the absence of definite instructions from our clients. If you desire to cover All Risks, we can provide such coverage at a slightly higher premium.

BREAKAGE: Breakage is a special risk, for which an extra premium is charged. The present rate is about . . . percent. Claims are payable for only part of the loss; that which is over 5% of the value.

VALUE TO BE INSURED: We note that you wish us to insure your shipments for 10% above invoice value, which is receiving our due attention.

We trust that the above information serves your purpose and await your further instructions.

Yours faithfully,

(Signature)

(2)

Gentlemen,

Re: Insurance under S/C No. 5468

Regarding S/C No. 5468 covering 5,000 tons of gum rosin of Chinese origin, we would like to inform you that we have established with the first National Bank of New York a confirmed, irrevocable L/C No. 7076 in the amount of $ . . . valid beginning October 25.

Please make sure that the above-mentioned goods are shipped before October 15 and insured against All Risks for 150% of invoice value. We know that your usual practice is to cover the goods only for 10% above invoice value and therefore, an extra premium will be needed for our account.

Please arrange the insurance as per our request and in the meantime we await your shipping advice.

Yours faithfully,

(Signature)

(3)

Dear Sirs,

In reply to your inquiry of May 15, we are prepared to cover the consignments in question. Considering our long-standing relationship, our insurance rate for Euro 100,000 A. R. policy on 2000 sets of GL Refrigerators from Zhuhai to the

Netherlands is 0. 5% of declared value.

This is our lowest rate. We hope you will be satisfied with it and give us the opportunity to handle your insurance business. We really hope our service will meet your needs.

Yours faithfully,

(Signature)

14. 4 Word study

(1) **In regard to**: in connection with or in relation to.
(2) **Cover**: to protect by insurance.
(3) **In the absence**: non-existence; lack.
(4) **Definite**: clearly known, seen, or stated, without any uncertainty.
(5) **Instruction**: advice on how to do something.
(6) **Desire**: to wish, to want, or hope for very much. *E. g.* We all desire happiness.
(7) **Coverage**: the amount of protection given by insurance; risks covered by insurance.
(8) **Premium**: a payment made to buy insurance, the fee charged by an insurance company is called the premium.
(9) **Breakage**: the cost of damage caused by broken things.
(10) **Payable**: must be paid.
(11) **Extra**: additionally; beyond what is usual or necessary.
(12) **Due**: proper, correct, or suitable.
(13) **Serve**: to be good enough or suitable for a purpose.
(14) **Await**: to wait for. *E. g.* I am awaiting your reply.
(15) **Gum rosin**: especially used in a solid form on the strings of a musical instrument. A thick sticky liquid that comes out of certain trees such as the fir; and later becomes a hard yellow substance. Gum rosin is used for making paint.
(16) **Invoice**: a detailed list of goods shipped or services rendered, with an accounting of all costs; an itemized bill, to make an invoice for goods or services. *E. g.* Sending an invoice to your customer.
(17) **Usual practice**: customary, in accordance with what happens or is done in

most cases.

(18) **Euro**: the basic monetary unit of most members of the European Union (introduced in 1999); in 2002 twelve European nations (Germany, France, Belgium, Luxembourg, the Netherlands, Italy, Spain, Portugal, Ireland, Greece, Austria, and Finland) adopted the Euro as their basic unit of money and abandoned their traditional currencies.

(19) **Duty**: something that one does either because it is part of one's job or because it is morally or legally right.

Cutural note:

The Netherlands: a constitutaonal monarchy in western Europe on the North Sea; achieved indepedndence from Spain in 1579; half the country lies below sea level.

14.5 Useful sentences

(1) In the absence of your detailed instructions, we will cover insurance WPA and War Risk according to our usual practice.

(2) Please cover us on the following goods.

(3) As you hold the policy, we should be grateful if you could take indemnification.

(4) We usually insure the goods sold on CIF basis with our underwriter.

(5) Many importers would like to be insured at this end with PICC.

(6) We would be grateful if you could quote a rate covering all risk from port to port.

(7) We have enclosed leaflets explaining our three fully comprehensive marine policies, which offer the sort of cover you required.

(8) We have covered insurance on the 100 metric tons of wool for 110% of the invoice value against All Risks.

(9) Insurance at a slightly higher premium, insurance with PICC.

(10) This insurance policy provides coverage against breakage.

(11) We hope no difficulty will arise in connection with the insurance claim and thank you in advance for your assistance.

(12) The insured goods are covered from the time when they leave the warehouse (at the place named in the policy for the commencement of the transit) and

continue to be covered until they are delivered to the final warehouse (at the destination named in the policy).

(13) The policy provides a prevailing time limit of 60 days after the completion of discharge of the insured goods from the sea going vessel at the final port of discharge.

(14) On the expiration of the time limit of 60 days, the coverage ceases to protect the goods even though they have not reached the final warehouse.

(15) The risks covered under the policy should be strictly in accordance with the terms of contract, or with those of the letter of credit, if shipment is made under this letter.

(16) We usually cover 110% of the invoice value against War Risk with PICC as per Chinese Marine Cargo Clauses of the PICC dated August 1st, 2011.

(17) Let us help you make those insurance decisions with a complimentary policy review.

(18) Many thanks for expressing your interest in my services. I realize that you have choices of many other agents and greatly appreciate the opportunity to fulfill your insurance needs.

(19) One of the best advantages of property insurance is that it offers something that is very hard to find.

(20) We enclose the surveyor's report and the shipping agent's statement. As our order was placed on a CIF basis and you covered the insurance, we would be grateful if you take this matter up with the insurers.

Unit 15 Shipment

15. 1 Introduction

Shipping is very important in foreign trade because goods sold need to be delivered to the buyer abroad, and the delivery of goods is made possible by shipping or transport services. The business of foreign trade shipping is complicated. Therefore, a good knowledge of the details regarding the procedures of shipment, and the shipping documents is needed to fulfill a transaction and effect shipment in a safe, accurate, and economical way. This unit discusses the letter content of shipping, types of shipment letters, notes to write, and sample letters.

15. 2 Letter content

The shipment clauses include the time of shipment, the ports of loading and destination, means of conveyance, and the shipping documents.

1) **Time of shipment**: refers to the time limit for loading the goods on board the vessel at the port of loading in line with the terms and conditions of the contract. The shipment should not take too long or too short after the contract is concluded. If a shipment is too early, the seller would not have enough time to get the goods ready. If it is made too late, the seller will have to wait quite a long time before he can receive payment.
2) **Port of loading and destination**: the former refers to the port of departure, while the latter refers to the destination that the goods are being shipped to. Generally, it is the seller who designates the port of shipment for the convenience of shipping the goods, while the buyer usually designates the port of destination.
3) **Means of conveyance**: covers direct shipment, trans-shipment and partial

shipment. In case of an export business covering a large amount of goods, it is necessary to make shipment in several lots by several carriers sailing on different dates. When there are no ships or few ships sailing directly to the port of destination, or the amount of cargo for a certain port of destination is so small that no ships would like to come at that port, trans-shipment is necessary. However, the buyer should allow partial shipment and trans-shipment in advance.

4) **Shipping documents**: the bill of lading, together with the insurance policy, commercial invoice, packing list, certificate of inspection, and certificate of origin constitutes the shipping documents.

15.3 Types of letters

Letters regarding shipment are usually written for the following purposes: to urge an early shipment; to amend shipping terms; to give shipping advice; to dispatch shipping documents, such as a shipping permit, shipping order, bill of lading and so on. Taking advantage of the occasion to advise the buyer of the shipment, the seller may also review the course of the transaction and express the desire for further development of business.

In the usual practice of international trade, under FOB terms, it is the buyer's responsibility to book the shipping space. The seller should send a notice to the buyer before the agreed shipment date (usually 30 – 45 days before shipping), so that the buyer can arrange the relevant vessel for accepting the delivery. The buyer, after receiving the relevant notice from the seller, should book the shipping space and notify the seller of the name of the vessel and the estimated arrival date of the vessel. Often in this notice, the buyer will instruct the seller to pay special attention to the delivery of the goods. This notice is often called "The Shipping Instruction".

Under FOB, especially under CFR, after the goods are placed onboard the vessel, the seller should notify the buyer of the contract number, the name and weight of the goods, the invoice amount, the vessel's name and the date of the shipment. Then the buyer can make necessary arrangements for purchasing the relevant insurance and receiving delivery of the goods. This notice sent by the seller to notify the delivery of the goods is called "Shipping Advice".

15. 4 Notes

When the shipment is completed, it signifies the seller's fulfillment of the obligation to make delivery of the goods. In foreign trade, shipment is mostly made by ocean vessels, tramp, or liner. A tramp is a freight-carrying vessel, which has no regular route or schedule of sailings; nor does it serve only one trade. It seeks out ports wherever there is a demand at the moment for shipping space. A liner is a vessel with regular sailings and arrivals on a stated schedule between specified ports.

To make a shipment by a liner, the first step is to ascertain the rate. The quotation of a rate for a specific shipment constitutes an offer on the part of the carrier. If the shipper wishes to make this rate binding, he must accept the proposal promptly at the rate quoted. The carrier then reserves the required space and delivers to the shipper or his agent a shipping permit, which is a shipping order. This permit is addressed to the receiving clerk at the dock. When the goods are delivered to the dock, the shipping permit is exchanged for a dock receipt or a mate's receipt, which is a brief statement from the carrier's representative at the dock, indicating that the shipment has been received in apparent good order. This is a temporary receipt that must be exchanged for the regular ocean bill of lading before the vessel sails.

The ocean bill of lading is an essential document when making a shipment. It represents three aspects. First, it is a receipt of the goods. Second, it is a contract for the performance of certain services with certain conditions. Third, it also serves as evidence of ownership of the goods described. When made out "to order", it becomes a negotiable instrument, used as security for loans and other purposes. When used in this way, it is known as an order bill of lading. The straight bill of lading, on the other hand, is made out to a specific consignee. Such a document is not negotiable.

After making shipment, the seller should promptly advise the buyer of its effectuation, no matter whether the transaction is concluded on FOB, or CFR basis. For FOB and CFR transactions, the buyer will have to provide insurance on the shipment upon receipt of shipping advice from the seller. It has been a customary practice that in the case of FOB transactions, the seller, before shipping, should ask the buyer to name the vessel on which the goods are to be shipped unless it is specified in the contract or L/C.

If the nature of the goods permit, and appropriate terms have been stipulated in the contract or L/C, the seller may choose to make several partial shipments of a given lot of contracted goods at different times. In cases where direct sailing from one port to the other is unavailable, trans-shipment is necessary. In order to avoid disputes that may arise in the future, the seller should first obtain consent from the buyer that the goods ordered might be sent to the port of destination by means of trans-shipment. As such, the stipulation "trans-shipment is allowed" should be stated in the L/C as well as in the contract. Instead of a bill of lading, an airway bill is used if goods are sent by air. Like a bill of lading, the airway bill serves as a receipt for the goods taken on board and is evidence of the contract terms regarding carriage. However, unlike the bill of lading, the airway bill is not a document of title. It cannot transfer ownership of the goods to which it refers.

15.5 Sample letters

(1) Urging the Shipment

Dear Sirs,

Re: Contract No. 4028

With reference to our previous letters and cables, we wish to call your attention to the fact that until now, we have received no news from you about the shipment in the captioned contract. We informed you in one of our previous letters that the users are in urgent need of the goods contracted and are in fact pressing us for assurance of an early delivery.

Under the circumstances, it is obviously impossible for us to again extend L/C No. 2237, which expires on November 18. We feel we should remind you about this matter again because prompt attention to this shipment is important to all parties concerned. We hope you will send us your shipping instructions without any further delay.

Yours truly,

(Signature)

(2) Shipping instruction

Gentlemen:

Re: Our Order No. 07659

Your S/C No. 1336

It is our pleasure to inform you that we have booked shipping space for the goods under the captioned order on the S. S. "Crown" which is scheduled to arrive at your port on or about the 28th of this month.

Please contact our shipping agents, Messrs Howard Vessel Co. Ltd., for loading arrangements and send us a confirmation when loading is completed.

Yours faithfully,

(Signature)

(3) Shipping documents

Dear Sirs,

We will ship the consignment on board S. S. "East Wind", which sails for your port tomorrow. The following documents are enclosed:

(1) One non-negotiable copy of bill of lading.

(2) Invoice in duplicate.

(3) Packing list in triplicate.

(4) One copy of makers' certificate of quality.

(5) One copy of insurance contract.

We hope the consignment will reach you on time, and meet your urgent needs.

Yours truly,

(Signature)

15.6 Word study

(1) **Shipment**: a load of goods sent together by sea, road, or air; the action of sending, carrying; or delivering goods. *E. g.* a large shipment of grain; The goods were ready for shipment.

(2) **Previous**: happening or existing before the one mentioned.

(3) **Contract**: a formal written agreement, having the force of law, between two

or more people or groups.

(4) **Expire**: something that lasts for a certain period of time; to come to an end; run out.

(5) **Assurance**: a firm statement that something is certainly true or will certainly happen; a promise.

(6) **Press**: to urge strongly.

(7) **Urgent**: very important and necessary to be dealt with quickly.

(8) **Extend**: to stretch out; to make longer or greater.

(9) **Circumstance**: the combination of facts, conditions, or events that influence your action, regarded as being outside your control.

(10) **Obviously**: easy to see and understand; clear; which must be recognized.

(11) **Instruction**: to give knowledge or information.

(12) **Crown**: a decorative covering for the head, usually made of gold and jewels, worn by a king or queen.

(13) **Space**: room to fit or accommodate something or somebody.

(14) **Schedule**: a list of times of departures and arrivals; a plan for performing work or achieving an objective, specifying the order and the allotting time for each part.

(15) **Contact**: to get in touch with; communicate with.

(16) **Load**: something that is to be carried, to put (a load) on or in (a vehicle).

(17) **Complete**: to finish, bring to an end, especially something that takes a long time.

(18) **Arrangement**: something that has been settled or agreed on.

(19) **Certificate**: formal declaration that documents a fact of relevance to finance and investment; the holder has a right to receive interest or dividends. *E. g.* He held several valuable securities.

(20) **Triplicate**: one of three copies; any of three things that correspond to one another exactly.

(21) **In line with**: comparing two values or ideas to one another. *E. g.* You can see our quote is in line with present market values.

(22) **Urge**: to suggest very strongly that something should be done.

15.7 Useful sentences

(1) We would like to inform you that the above goods were shipped on the 18th of May.

(2) We have the pleasure to confirm our fax, informing you that we have shipped the following goods by M/S "Pacific Bear" of the U. S. Lines which left here today.

(3) We wish to advise you that, in accordance with your esteemed order of April 20, 2004, we shipped the goods to you today by S. S. "Tokyo Maru". We are confident that your order for 50 cases of carbon paper will reach you on time and in good condition.

(4) We take pleasure in notifying you that the goods under S/C 456 have been dispatched by M/V "Greenwood" sailing on May 15, 2004 for Hong Kong.

(5) We wish to inform you that we have shipped the following goods by S. S. "Shanghai" according to your instructions of August 5.

(6) We wish to advise you that the goods under S/C No. 234 were dispatched on the steamer "Yunnan" in July, and are expected to reach your port in early September. We trust the goods will reach you safely.

(7) The shipment of chemical fertilizer under Contract No. 2346 will be effected by S. S. "Calchas", which is scheduled to leave here on July 16th.

(8) Enclosed you will find copies of the shipping documents.

(9) Enclosed please find copies of the bill of lading, the invoice, and the insurance policy covering the shipment.

(10) The goods we ordered are seasonal goods, so it will be better to ship them all at one time.

(11) We hope the goods will arrive in time for the New Year's rush.

(12) We hope that you will make all necessary arrangements to deliver the goods on time.

(13) The first lot will be delivered by June. You will receive the remainder by the end of the year.

(14) We are willing to pay an additional fee for immediate delivery.

(15) It is now over two months since we sent in the order for Tape Recorders, yet we are still awaiting delivery. Please remember that the delivery date is of

utmost importance to us.

(16) Please look into this matter immediately and make sure that the goods are delivered without further delay.

(17) Please make your best effort to dispatch the goods with the least possible delay.

(18) We are greatly in need of the goods. Please expedite our shipment as soon as possible.

(19) If the shipment does not arrive on time, we may refuse it.

(20) If you fail to make delivery within the stipulated time, we will have to lodge a claim against you for our losses and reserve the right to cancel the contract.

(21) We regret to inform you that unless you give us the notification of the delivery of the goods within the next two weeks, we shall be obliged to cancel the order. Please make this matter your top priority.

(22) We wish to point out that if you fail to achieve shipment within the time specified, we will not be able to fulfill our contracts with our clients.

(23) We would like to emphasize that any delay in shipping our order will undoubtedly cause us major complications.

(24) Your failure to deliver the goods within the stipulated time has greatly inconvenienced us.

(25) Besides the above mentioned surcharges, sometimes the ice surcharge, cleaning tank surcharge, and currency adjustment factor fumigation surcharge, etc. are included.

(26) We hereby inform you that the goods under the above mentioned credit have been shipped.

(27) The details of the shipment are stated below.

(28) Shipment shall be effected at internals of every other month.

(29) Shipment will be spread over 3 months, starting in March.

(30) The packing of your last shipment left much to be desired.

Unit 16 Container Service

16.1 Introduction

With the expansion of international trade, container service has become popular. The use of containers provides a highly efficient form of transport by road, rail, and air. However, their fullest benefits are felt in shipping, where costs may be reduced by as much as half. Containers are constructed of metal and are of standard lengths ranging from ten to forty feet. There are several topics in this unit: the advantages of container service, packing methods, the way to mark, and sample letters.

16.2 Advantages of container service

This service has the following advantages:

1) Containers can be loaded and locked at factory premises or at nearby container bases, making pilferage impossible.
2) There is no risk of goods getting lost or mislaid in transit.
3) Manpower in handling is greatly reduced, with lower costs and lower risk of damage.
4) Mechanical handling enables cargoes to be loaded in a matter of hours rather than days; thus reducing the time ships spend in port and greatly increasing the number of sailings.
5) Temperature-controlled containers are provided for the types of cargo that need them.

16. 3 Packing

We all know that packing is an art, and that the real art of packing is to get the contents into a nice, compact shape that will stay that way during the roughest journey. Because packing has become more important during modern trade activities, the seller should pay much attention to the features, appearance, and packaging methods.

First, the basic purpose is to protect the product. This is important because the product may have to withstand a lot of handling during transportation between the factory and the consumer. The second purpose of packaging is to make the product look appealing to the buyer. Products that are packed in such a way as to catch the consumer's eyes will help to sell. Third, other common purposes of packing are to provide information about the product inside, make it easy to carry the product, and provide convenience in using the product.

The features of packing should be:

1) Beautiful and durable.

2) Easy to handle.

3) Well-suited for long distance shipment.

4) Insurance against damage.

5) Waterproof and shakeproof.

6) Standardized.

The appearance and packaging of packing should:

1) Be modern and attractive.

2) Be small and exquisite.

3) Be suitable for window display.

4) Facilitate marketing in supermarkets, etc.

In addition to adding to the attractiveness of the commodities, good packaging can also appeal to the customers and can help push sales.

We often use one or some of the packing containers: bag, sack, carton, case, box, crate, drum, bale, can, carboy, bundle, container, pallet.

16. 4 Marking

After finishing packing according to the packing instructions from the buyer, marking should be done on the export packages. There are three major types of marking: first, the consignee's own distinctive marks which includes the name of the port of destination.

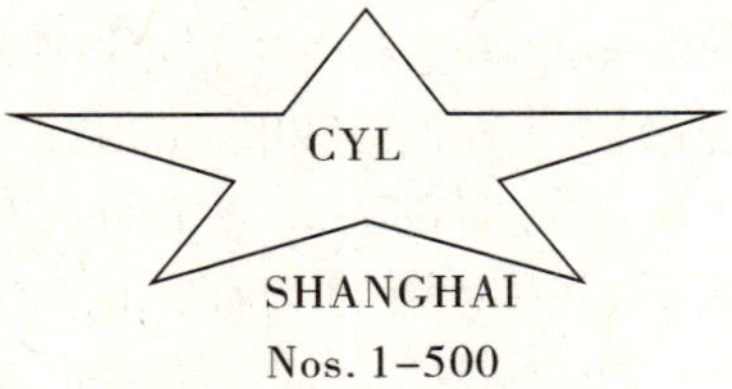

Some patterns of marks often used in international trade include the followings:

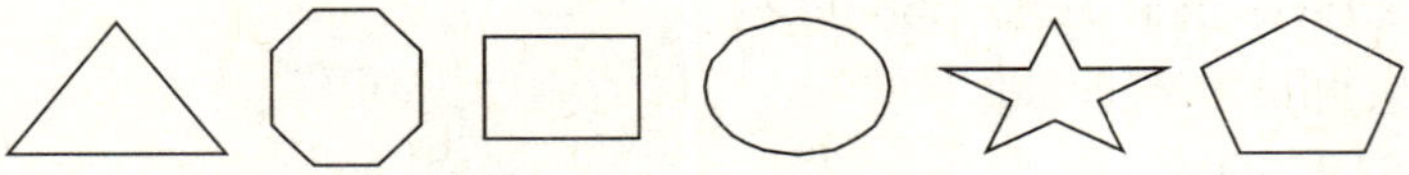

Second, a certain official mark required by authorities. Some countries require the name of the origin country, and weight, size, and some dimensions to be added on the package.

IRAN	100cm × 50cm × 50cm
Nos. 1 – 150	Gross weight: 60 kilos
MADE IN CHINA	net weight: 53. 5 kilos

Third kind of marking is special directions or warnings. Sometimes specific instructions regarding manner of handling, loading, lifting, etc., may be needed. Various warnings are to be stenciled on the packages for the benefit of all parties involved.

THIS SIDE UP
USE NO HOOKS
KEEP DRY
TOP
PERISHABLE
INFLAMMABLE
LIFT HERE
ACID—HANDLE WITH CARE
GLASS—HANDLE WITH CARE
FRAGILE
TO BE KEPT COOL
STOW AWAY FROM HEAT
DO NOT DROP
DO NOT STOW ON DECK
OPEN THIS END
HANDLE WITH CARE

16. 5 Sample letters

(1) Packing instructions

Dear Sirs,

We assume that by now you have received our order No. 0543 for large tins of paint. Now we must give you our packing instructions for the order in question. As you know, paint is a highly inflammable commodity, and extra precautions are necessary. We would like you to pack the goods in strong metal cases, each containing 40 tins. Please see to it that each case is properly sealed, with a fireproof lining inside.

We trust you will act in accordance with these instructions.

Yours faithfully,

(Signature)

(2) Shipping marks

Dear Sirs,

Thank you for your letter of April 10, which included sample towels. Enclosed is our contract No. AD-168 ordering 7,000 dozen "Yongliang" towels.

This is the first transaction between us, and we would like to make it clear in advance that all the towels are to be packed in poly bags of one piece each; 10 dozen of solid color and assorted sizes to a carton lined with waterproof paper. To protect the goods from any possible damage in transit, please make sure that the cartons are reinforced by double plastic straps. The shipping mark and indicative mark,

"Handle with Care" is to be stenciled on the outer packing as follows:

DG

SC989642

LC886535 HANDLE WITH CARE

LONDON

CTN/No. 1-UP

We hope the above requirements are met exactly as requested.

Yours faithfully,

(Signature)

(3) Packing for dangerous goods

Dear Mr. Tanaka,

Your consignment of chemicals is now ready for dispatch and we are arranging shipment by S. S. Yamaha Maru, sailing from Shanghai on May 24.

The sulfuric acid is supplied in thirty 4-gallon carboys, double-packed for extra safety, and with a protective lid to avoid breakage. The ammonia is in forty 5-cwt steel drums.

Please confirm the safe arrival of the consignment.

Yours faithfully,

(Signature)

16.6 Word study

(1) **Assume**: taken to be the case, or to be true; accept without verification or proof. *E. g.* I assume his train was late.

(2) **Inflammable**: possible to burn.

(3) **Precaution**: a precautionary measure warding off impending danger or damage or injury etc. *E. g.* He put an ice pack on the injury as a precaution.

(4) **Seal**: fastener consisting of a resinous composition that is plastic when warm; used for sealing documents and parcels and letters.

(5) **Waterproof**: make resistant to water, sound, or errors, etc. *E. g.* Waterproof the materials against shrinking in the dryer.

(6) **Transaction**: the act of transacting within or between groups as carrying on commercial activities. *E. g.* No transactions are possible without him; He has

always been honest is his transactions with me.

(7) **Assort**: arrange or order by classes or categories. *E. g.* How would you assort these pottery shards—are they prehistoric?

(8) **Carton**: a box made of cardboard; opens by flaps on top.

(9) **Reinforce**: strengthen and support with rewards. *E. g.* Let's reinforce good behavior.

(10) **Strap**: an elongated leather strip or strip of similar material for binding things together or holding something in position.

(11) **Transit**: a journey usually by ship. *E. g.* His outward passage took 10 days transit.

(12) **Stencil**: a thin sheet of material with a shape cut out of it through which paint or ink is applied to mark a shape or lettering on another surface.

(13) **Chemical**: relating to or used in chemistry. *E. g.* chemical engineer; chemical balance.

(14) **Dispatch**: the act of sending off something.

(15) **Sulfuric**: of or relating to or containing sulfur. *E. g.* sulphuric esters.

(16) **Gallon**: a British imperial capacity measure (liquid or dry) equal to 4 quarts or 4. 545 liters; the United States liquid unit equal to 4 quarts or 3. 785 liters.

(17) **Lid**: a movable top or cover (hinged or separate) for closing the opening of a container.

(18) **Ammonia**: a pungent gas compound of nitrogen and hydrogen (NH_3).

16. 7 Useful sentences

(1) It has been estimated that as much as 70% of all cargo losses could be prevented by proper packaging and marking.

(2) 5000 pieces per carton; carton size is 37cm ×77cm ×25 cm, based on the products' G. W.

(3) This paper sheet is made of recycled material, which is environmentally friendly. It's very popular in the market place. It can be used for packaging of shoes, gifts, etc.

(4) Each pair of nylon socks is packed in a poly-bag and there are 12 pairs in a box.

(5) Pens are packed 12 pieces to a box and 200 boxes to a wooden case.

(6) Please mark the cases with our initials in a diamond, under which comes the destination with contract number.

(7) The inner packing must be beautiful, attractive, and helpful for sales.

(8) The goods are to be packed in a container that contains 20 boxes.

(9) The new packing of the dresses is British-style and suitable for the European market.

(10) Packing charges are excluded in the quoted price.

(11) The packing must be strong enough to stand rough handling.

(12) The name of the country or trademark must appear on the outside of the container.

(13) The goods will be shipped soon; we hope each box will be marked with net weight, warnings, and direction.

(14) This packing is waterproof and shockproof; we use some warnings, such as "do not drop", or "fragile".

(15) Cartons are widely used in international trade; do not worry about it.

(16) The quality is much higher than that of similar goods on the market, but the packing is poorer; therefore, please change the shipping container.

(17) In order to promote our sales, please use thinner and more colorful paper for our future goods.

(18) The packing described above is seaworthy export packing and fits for long distance ocean transportation.

(19) We have received your letter of August 11th concerning the packing details; we are pleased to acknowledge them as follows.

(20) Please mark the containers with the name of origin country, tare, new weight, and a warning, "do not use hook".

Unit 17 Payment

17. 1 Introduction

Payment plays an important role in foreign trade. It is often complicated. The method of payment for each transaction is to be agreed upon between the two trading parties at the time an order is placed. The most often adopted mode of payment in foreign trade is the Letter of Credit (L/C). According to the Uniform Customs and Practice for Documentary Credits, documentary credit means any arrangement whereby the bank (the issuing bank) acts at the request and on the instructions of a customer (the applicant) or on its own behalf.

There are various types of L/C, such as irrevocable documentary credit; revolving credit; standby credit, and back-to-back credit. The parties involved in a documentary credit are: the applicant (importers or buyers), the issuing bank, the advising bank, the confirming banks, if any, the nominated paying or negotiating/accepting bank, and the beneficiary (seller or exporter).

The topics discussed in this unit are: the procedures for issuing a letter of credit; the content of a L/C; urging the establishment of L/C; L/C amendments and extensions; and sample letters.

17. 2 The procedures for issuing L/C

First, the buyer and the seller make a sales contract, choose the method of payment by documentary credit. Second, the buyer informs his or her bank, the "issuing bank", to open a credit and make the seller as the beneficiary. Third, the issuing bank contacts another bank, usually in the country of the seller, to advise and perhaps to add its confirmation to the documentary credit. Finally, the advising or confirming bank informs the seller that the credit has been issued.

As you can see from the above procedures the service of the banks is very important.

17. 3 The content of a L/C

The letter of credit includes 17 parts, but not all the parts are necessary. They are: issuing bank; issuing date; expiry date and expiry place; applicant; beneficiary; documentary credit number; currency code and amount; description of goods and/or service; documents required clause; price terms; shipment date; period for presentation of documents; reimbursing bank; reimbursement clause; banking charges clause; valid conditions clause; special conditions.

A letter of credit must bear a valid period, which may be longer than the shipping period. The shipping date should not be later than the validity date of the letter of credit. If validity is not stated in the credit, the validity of credit shall be determined according to the shipping date.

The description of commodities in a commercial invoice must correspond with that in the credit. In all other documents, the goods may be described in general terms, not inconsistent with that of the goods in the credit. The words "about", "approximately", "circa" or similar expression used in connection with the amount of the credit, or the quantity, or the unit price stated in the credit are to be construed as allowing a difference not to exceed 10% more or less than the amount, quantity or unit price to which they refer.

In addition to stipulating an expiry date for presentation of documents, every credit which calls for a transport document should also stipulate a specified period of time after the date of shipment during which presentation must be made in compliance with terms and conditions of the credit. If no such period is stipulated, banks will not accept documents presented to them later than 21 days after the date of shipment.

In any event, documents must be presented not later than the expiry date of the credit. The letter of credit is opened on the basis of the contract, but it is independent from the contract once it is opened. The bank is only bound by, and makes payment against documents, which are fully in conformity with the credit. L/C business is purely the business of documents handling, under which the bank is not responsible for the goods, but only for the documents. The documents presented by the exporter must be in strict conformity with the credit, otherwise the bank has the right to reject them.

17. 4 Urging the establishment of L/C

When a transaction is made, it is the buyer's obligation to establish L/C with his or her bank within the validity of the contract. It is usual practice in export trade that the L/C should be established and to be in the hands of the seller one month prior to the date of the shipment. This gives the seller enough time for shipping preparation. **For example**, making the goods ready and booking shipping space. For prompt shipment, the L/C should be transmitted by email or fax immediately after the transaction is made.

If the buyer fails to establish the L/C, or the L/C does not reach the seller on time; the seller can send a letter by email or fax to the buyer urging him to expedite the L/C. If this situation arises, it is advisable that the seller should keep his calm, not show anger or unhappiness, and write a reasonable letter. The first message sent, should be a polite note saying that the goods ordered are ready for shipment but the relevant L/C has not been received. If the seller does not get any response, then he can send another letter to express disappointment, still keep being polite and restrained.

The purpose of a letter urging the establishment of L/C is to persuade the buyer to fulfill his or her part of the agreement. This type of letter should be written with consideration and respect.

17. 5 L/C amendments and extensions

After receiving the relevant L/C, the seller should make a thorough examination of the documents. He should make sure that all the clauses set forth in the L/C are in full conformity with the terms stated in the sales contract. Otherwise the seller might suffer a great deal of inconveniences if there are any discrepancies between the L/C and the contract. The negotiating bank may refuse negotiation of the document. So if the seller sees something wrong in the L/C, he should send a notice to the buyer immediately, asking him to make adjustments. If there is an unexpected situation with the supply, shipment, etc., then an amendment to the L/C is needed.

Both the seller and the buyer can ask for amendments to the L/C. The usual procedure is that the buyer asks consent from the seller and then informs the opening bank to change the L/C.

Sometimes, the seller may fail to get the goods ready for shipment on time or the buyer may request that the shipment be postponed for some reason. In that case, the seller should ask for an extension to the expiration date as well as the date of the shipment on the L/C. This kind of letter is often made by email or fax.

17.6 Sample letters

(1) D/A and D/P terms

Dear Sirs,

Thank you for your letter of May 18. We have carefully studied your proposal for payment by D/A for a trial order of T-shirts. We regret that we are unable to entertain your request.

Our usual practice is to require payment by confirmed and irrevocable letter of credit. That is to say, at present, we cannot accept D/A terms in none of transactions with our buyers abroad. However, considering the friendly nature of our relationship, we are (only in this exception), prepared to accept D/P at sight.

We sincerely hope that the above payment terms are acceptable to you and trust you will recognize the value of our cooperation.

Looking forward to your earliest reply.

Sincerely yours,

(Signature)

(2) Establishment of L/C

Dear Sirs,

We write to inform you that we have now opened the confirmed, irrevocable letter of credit No. 56781 in your favor for US $60,000 with the Bank of China, London, valid until June 30th.

As the busy season is drawing near, our buyers are in urgent need of the goods. Please arrange shipment of the goods ordered by us upon receipt of the L/C. We would like to stress that any delay in shipping our order will place us in a difficult position. We hope that you will let us know at your earliest convenience the name of the carrying vessel and its sailing date.

Thank you for your cooperation.

Yours faithfully,

(Signature)

(3) Amendment to L/C.

Dear Sirs,

Re: Letter of Credit No. 65290

We thank you for your L/C No. 65290 covering your order No. EX-25 for 10,000 waterproof raincoats.

We have noticed that in the L/C you have forgotten to mention that the quality of the goods is to be based on the certificate of quality issued by the China Commodity Inspection Bureau, as you agreed upon when placing the order.

On the contrary, you have inserted two clauses to the effect that inspection of the goods will be made at the port of destination and that you have the right to lodge claims against us within 10 days after the arrival of the shipment.

We believe that this discrepancy perhaps has escaped your attention and we regret to say that we cannot agree to such terms. Your prompt amendment to the L/C and deletion of the two clauses are urgently requested.

Yours faithfully,

(Signature)

(4) Letter of credit

Dear Sirs,

We hereby issue the Irrevocable Documentary Letter of Credit, which is available by beneficiary's drafts on us for full invoice value at sight bearing the credit number and date of issue, and accompanied by the following documents:

(1) Signed Commercial Invoice in quintuplicate.

(2) Canadian Customs Invoice in quintuplicate.

(3) Packing list in quintuplicate.

(4) Weight and Measurement Certificate in quintuplicate.

(5) Full set of clean onboard Bills of Lading issued by order of shipper marked "freight prepaid" and notify the accountee.

(6) Evidencing shipment of: about 300, 000 yards of 65% Polyester, 35% Cotton Grey Lawn as per buyers orders No. S-0578.

(7) CFR Montreal.

We are informed that insurance is to be covered by the buyer.

Shipment from China to Montreal Latest July 31, 2012	Partial shipment permitted
	Trans-shipment permitted

All other bank charges are for the account of beneficiary. Documents must be presented to negotiating bank or paying bank within 15 days after the onboard date of Bills of Lading, but within validity of Letter of Credit.

Special Conditions: two sets of non-negotiable shipping documents must be airmailed directly to Kanematsu-Gosho Inc. , Montreal, Canada. A beneficiary's certificate to this effect is required.

Special instructions for reimbursement: we will pay the negotiating bank as per their instructions upon receipt of documents. The amount of any draft drawn under this credit must, concurrently with negotiation, be endorsed on the reverse hereof, and the presentation of any such draft shall be a warranty by the negotiating bank that such endorsement has been made and that documents have been forwarded as herein required.

We hereby engage with the drawers, endorsers, and bona fide holders of drafts drawn and negotiated under and in compliance with the terms of this credit that the same shall be duly honored on due presentation to the drawer.

The advising bank is requested to notify the beneficiary without adding their confirmation.

Yours faithfully,

(Signature)

THE BANK OF TOKYO, LTD.

17. 7 Word study

(1) **Entertain**: take into consideration; have in view. *E. g.* He entertained the idea of moving to South America.

(2) **Exception**: a deliberate act of omission. *E. g.* With the exception of the children, everyone was told the news.

(3) **Stress**: special emphasis attached to something. *E. g.* The stress was more on accuracy than on speed.

(4) **Raincoat**: a water-resistant coat.

(5) **Inspection**: a formal or official examination. *E. g.* The platoon stood ready for inspection; We had to wait for the inspection before we could use the elevator.

(6) **Bureau**: an administrative unit of a government. *E. g.* the Census Bureau.

(7) **Insert**: a folded section placed between the leaves of another publication.

(8) **Lodge**: file a formal charge against; register complaint or appeal. *E. g.* The suspect was lodged with murdering his wife.

(9) **Discrepancy**: a difference between conflicting facts or claims or opinions.

(10) **Escape**: the act of escaping physically. *E. g.* He made his escape from the mental hospital; The canary escaped from its cage; His escape was an indication of his guilt.

(11) **Amendment**: a statement that is added to or revises or improves a proposal or document.

(12) **Freight**: the charge for transporting something by common carrier. *E. g.* We pay the freight; The freight rate is usually cheaper.

(13) **Polyester**: a complex ester used for making fibers or resins or plastics or as a plasticizer.

(14) **Partial**: being or affecting only a part; not total. *E. g.* a partial description of the suspect; partial collapse; a partial eclipse; a partial monopoly; partial immunity.

(15) **Reimbursement**: compensation paid (to someone) for damages or losses or money already spent etc. *E. g.* He received reimbursement for his travel expenses.

(16) **Concurrently**: overlapping in duration.

(17) **Warranty**: a written assurance that some product or service will be provided or will meet certain specifications.

(18) **Endorsement**: formal and explicit approval. *E. g.* A Democrat usually gets the union's endorsement.

(19) **Validity**: having legal force; effective or binding.

(20) **Agree to it**: make sure that.

Cultural note:

Montreal, Canada

Montreal is a city in southern Quebec province on the Saint Lawrence River; the largest city in Quebec and second largest in Canada; the second largest French-speaking city in the world.

17.8 Useful sentences

(1) Payment is to be made by confirmed and irrevocable L/C for 100% invoice value available by sight draft accompanied with shipping documents.

(2) We are pleased to learn that you have opened a L/C with the Frank Bank in London, in favor of Messrs. Bush & Co., for the amount of US $200,000 available until November 20.

(3) The L/C should remain valid for negotiation in China within 15 day after the month of shipment.

(4) We have repeatedly requested you to expedite the issuing of the letter of credit so that the delivery process can proceed. Regrettably, one month has elapsed and we have not heard from you.

(5) The credit is short by the amount of US $66,000 and we must ask you to amend the amount immediately.

(6) Please amend the letter of credit reading "Partial Shipment Allowed".

(7) Please extend the shipment date until the end of September 2005. Please see to it that the amendment advice reaches us before August 31, without which you must extend the authority of the letter of credit until the end of November.

(8) Within 30 days after we have accepted your order, you are to open a confirmed and irrevocable letter of credit payable by T/T against presentation of shipping documents to the local branch of the Bank of China at the port of shipment.

(9) We will draw on your documentary draft at sight, on a collection basis, without a L/C.

(10) D/P will be accepted if the amount is under US $5,000.

(11) In view of the small amount involved in this transaction, we agree to draw on you through a bank at site for the value of the goods ordered.

(12) It is necessary that relevant credit should be established in strict accordance with the stipulations of our contract in order to avoid unnecessary

amendments.

(13) I send you here with a check, in the amount of US $250, 000. Please acknowledge the receipt by return mail.

(14) We are duly in receipt of your acceptance of the May 5th invoice, and have enclosed a draft US $51, 250 for payment of the balance of your account.

(15) Kindly draw the amount of your invoice on Messrs. A & Co. of Hamburg, three months from today, and include a bill of lading, requesting them to generate the insurance.

(16) I take liberty to trouble you with the enclosed draft for US $6, 000 on Mr. Smith, at thirty days sight, which I hope you will accept and retain in your possession until due; at which time you can remit the amount to me.

(17) Your draft dated the 7th of October, will be honored at 30 days from the date to your order.

(18) We hereby engage in business with the drawers, endorsers, and bona-fide holders of the draft drawn under and in compliance with the terms of credit. That such draft shall be duly honored on presentation and delivery of documents as specified, if drawn and negotiated within the dates of this credit.

(19) A copy of this cable must accompany the documents for negotiation.

(20) All documents except bills of lading are to be made out to ABC Co. Ltd. , whose name is to be on the bill of lading as joint notifying party with the applicant.

Unit 18 Sales Contract

18. 1 Introduction

A contract is an agreement between two or more parties that is enforceable in a court of law. In international trade, a sales contract comes into existence through a chain of correspondence between the exporter and importer. This unit discusses the content of the contract, types of comtracts, and sample letters.

18. 2 Content of the contract

Sales contracts, in their simplest form, are accepted orders or offers. For large and complicated sales, a detailed contract must be carefully drawn up and signed by the two business parties. It is important that the contract is negotiated with care so that both the buyer and seller are willing and able to live within its terms, and know clearly and unambiguously what is expected of them.

Traditional sales contracts include the followings:

1) Name and address of the seller and buyer.

2) The willingness and guarantee of both sides to carry out the contract.

3) Name, model, quality, quantity, and packing of the goods.

4) Price.

5) Terms of payment.

6) Time of shipment.

7) Shipping terms.

8) Port of loading and port of destination.

And some other items, such as insurance, the documents required by the buyer, quality/quantity discrepancy and claims, force majeure, arbitration, remarks, signatures.

18. 3 Types of contracts

The importer may come in with an initial inquiry requesting a price quotation for a certain type of quantity of merchandise. The seller, in turn, responds with the desired information. Usually, this response can already by interpreted as an offer that is binding on the exporter, provided the importer accepts it within a reasonable period of time. After many rounds of negotiation, when the buyer effectively accepts an actual offer, the transaction is completed and a contractual relationship between the buyer and seller is concluded.

International business is much more complicated than domestic business, thus detailed contracts and documents are indispensable. A contract is made to further specify the rights and obligations of both sides for legal purposes. Should any conflict between the two sides arise later, reference is generally made to the contract in an effort to resolve the misunderstanding. The commonly used forms of contracts are the formal contract, confirmation, agreement, and memorandum.

The various documents used in international business fall into four categories, which are: commercial documents, financial documents, official documents, and other certificates. In some cases, the narrow sense of documents is used. It simply stands for shipping documents.

18. 4 Sample letters

(1)

Sales Confirmation

China National Chemical Import and Export Corporation
Guangdong Branch
678 . . . Road
Guangzhou, China
Cable Address: SINOCHEMIC No.
Telex: 44076 HACON CN Date

SALES CONFIRMATION

Your cable/Letter
Our cable/Letter

To Messrs.

Dear Sirs,

We hereby confirm having sold to you the following goods on terms and conditions as stipulated below:

(1) Name of Commodity and Specification, Packing and Shipping Marks.

(2) Quantity.

(3) Unit Price.

(4) Total Amount (Quantity More or Less allowed . . . %).

(5) Time of Shipment: within . . . days after receipt of L/C allowing transshipment and partial shipment.

(6) Terms of payment: By 100% confirmed, irrevocable, transferable and divisible letter of credit to be available by sight draft and to remain valid for negotiation in China until 10 days after the afore said time of shipment.

(7) Insurance: Covers All Risk only to be effected by the buyer.

IMPORTANCE NOTICE

When opening L/C, please mention our S/C number.

REMARKS:

(1) The Buyer shall establish the covering L/C before . . . If this does not happen, the Seller reserves the right to rescind without further notice, to accept the whole or any part of this Sales Confirmation unfulfilled by the Buyer, or to lodge a claim for direct losses sustained, if any. For transactions concluded on CIF basis, it is understood that the insurance amount will be for 110% of the invoice value against the risks specified in the Sales Confirmation. If additional insurance amount or coverage is required, the buyer must have the consent of the Seller before shipment, and the additional premium is to be borne by the Buyer.

(2) Quality/Quantity Discrepancy: In case of quality discrepancy, a claim should be filed by the Buyer within 30 days after the arrival of the goods at port of destination; while for quantity discrepancy, claim should be filed by the Buyer within 15 days after the arrival of the goods at port of destination. It is understood that the Seller shall not be liable for any discrepancy of the goods shipped, due to causes

for which the Insurance Company, Shipping Company, other transportation organization or Post Office is liable.

(3) The Seller shall not be held liable for failure or delay in delivery of the entire lot or a portion of the goods under this Sales Confirmation in consequence of any Force Majeure incidents.

(4) The Buyer is requested always to quote the number of the sales confirmation in the L/C to be opened in favor of the Seller.

(5) The Buyer is requested to sign and return one copy of this Sales Confirmation immediately after the receipt of the same. Objection, if any, should be raised by the Buyer within five days after the receipt of this Sales Confirmation, in the absence of which it is understood that the Buyer has accepted the terms and conditions of the Sales Confirmation.

(2)

Date

Dear Sirs,

Thank you for your acceptance confirmation of Jan 18th. We are pleased to send you our sales confirmation No. 96DRA207 for your signing.

Portable Mixer Pm-23 $23FOB Dalian/Set 100 Sets $2300. 00

Vacuum cleaner Vc-18 $47FOB Dalian/Set 100 Sets $4700. 00

Terms: As usual

We hope that the goods will be shipped by June 30th, and we ensure the L/C will reach you no later than April 30.

Yours Faithfully,

(Signature)

Buyers: DAEHO APPAREL CO. LTD.
C. P. O. BOX 7155 SEOUL, KOREA

Sellers: DALIAN TEXTILES IMPORT & EXPORT CORP.
4 YING CHUN STREET, DALIAN, CHINA

18. 5 Word study

(1) **Contract**: a binding agreement between two or more people that is enforceable by law.

(2) **Specify**: to state exactly, describe fully.

(3) **Negotiable**: able to be negotiated or arranged by compromise. *E. g.* Negotiable demands; The proposal is still negotiable on the table.

(4) **Stipulate**: specify as a condition or requirement in a contract or agreement; make an express demand or provision in an agreement. *E. g.* The contract will stipulates that she can live in the house for the rest of her life; The contract stipulates the dates of the payments.

(5) **Trans-shipment**: the transfer from one conveyance to another for shipment.

(6) **Transferable**: capable of being moved or conveyed from one place to another.

(7) **Divisible**: capable of being or liable to be divided or separated. *E. g.* Even numbers are divisible by two; The Americans fought a bloody war to prove that their nation is not divisible.

(8) **Rescind**: annul by recalling or rescinding. *E. g.* He revoked the ban on smoking; lift an embargo; vacate a death sentence.

(9) **Consent**: permission to do something. *E. g.* He indicated his consent.

(10) **Destination**: the place designated as the end (as of a race or journey). *E. g.* A crowd assembled at the finish line; He was nearly exhausted as their destination came into view.

(11) **Liable**: legally responsible. *E. g.* If the merchandise arrives damaged, you are liable and will have to pay the damage. **liable to**: at risk of or subject to experiencing something usually unpleasant. *E. g.* He is apt to lose; She is liable to forget.

(12) **Portable**: an item that can easily be carried.

(13) **Textile**: material made by weaving or felting or knitting or crocheting from natural or synthetic fibers. *E. g.* Woven textile originated in Mesopotamia around 5000 BC; She measured off enough textile for a dress.

18. 6 Useful sentences

(1) This agreement is entered into effect on December 10th, 2003 through amicable negotiations between ×× Company, ×× (country) (hereinafter called Party A) and ××× Enterprise, ××× (country) (hereinafter called Party B) on the basis of equality and mutual benefit to develop business on the following terms.

(2) This contract is made and entered into by and between ×× Company, ×× (country) and ××× Enterprise, ××× (country).

(3) Not withstanding any other provisions to the contrary herein, insurance coverage and limits shall be subject to approval of all the parties.

(4) The Seller is liable for any damage of the goods and the expenses caused by improper packing, as well as for any rust attributed to inadequate or improper protective measures taken by the Seller in regard to the packing.

(5) Signed commercial invoice in quadruplicate certified to be true and correct stating full name and address of manufacturers.

(6) Full set of clean on board ocean bill of lading marked "freight collect" issued by shipping company, made out to order of shippers and endorsed in black.

(7) A separate Certificate of Origin was issued by the China Council for the Promotion of International Trade.

(8) This credit is valid until November 30, 2000 for presentation of documents in Kuwait.

(9) We guarantee the payment of drafts drawn in conformity with the terms and conditions stated.

(10) The negotiating bank must send all documents including the drafts directly to us, and the originals by registered airmail.

(11) This L/C is subject to Unit Form Customs and Practice for Documentary Credit, 2009 Revision of International Chamber of Commerce, Publication No. 500.

(12) If one side fails to observe the contract, the other side is entitled to cancel it.

(13) Please sign a copy of our Sales Contract No. 515515 enclosed here in triplicate and return it to us for our file.

(14) This contract is made out in two originals: English and Chinese. Both versions are equally valid.

(15) If shipment is delayed because the buyer fails to furnish proof in a timely manner, the seller will not be deemed to have breached the contract.

(16) It is agreed that the parties have to consider what would be a reasonable estimate of the damages they would suffer if the other were to breach this agreement.

(17) All the activities of both parties shall comply with the contractual stipulations.

(18) Both parties agree to change the time of shipment to June, and change terms of the currency from U. S. dollars to Euro.

References

[1] Cheng Tongchun. *International Business Correspondence in English.* Southeast University Press, 2001.

[2] Zou Xiurong. *International Business Correspondence in English.* Jiangxi University Press, 2010.

[3] Lei Chunlin. *Business English Writing.* University of International Business and Economic Press, 2008.

[4] Jiang Xianqiong. *Business English Correspondence.* Jilin University Press, 2005.

[5] Guan Guocai, Kong Zhimin, Wang Yuan. *Foreign Business Correspondence.* Tsinghua University & Beijing Transport University Press, 2010.

[6] Teng Meirong. *English for International Business Communication.* Capital University of Economics Press, 2005.

[7] Bao Jinling. *Business English Correspondence.* University of International Business & Economics Press, 2008.

[8] Gan Hong. *English Letter for International Business Communication.* Shanghai Science and Technology Literature Publishing House Press, 1996.

[9] Li Yajing. *English Correspondence on International Trade and Economics.* Qingdao Ocean Publisher Press, 1997.

[10] Guo Jirong, Hong Xinfa. *Business Correspondence and Communication in English.* Xi'an JiaoTong University Press, 2008.

[11] He Weixiang. *Business Writing in English.* Zhongshan University Press, 2001.

[12] Li Yajing, Li Yongfang, Zhang Deyu. *English Correspondence on International Trade and Economics.* Qingdao Ocean University Press, 1997.

[13] Wang Naiyan. *Business English Correspondence.* University of International Business and Economic Press, 2001.

[14] Liang Xiaoling. *International Business Correspondence in English.* University of International Business and Economics Press, 2005.

[15] Liu Huiling, Wang Jun. *International Business Correspondence.* University

of International Business and Economic Press, 2002.

[16] Wang Xiaoying. *A Writing Course for Business English*. Southeast University Press, 2004.

[17] Xie Long cheng. *Business English Communications*. Tourism Education Press, 1993.

[18] Chen Yongsheng. *Practical International Business and Trade Correspondence in English*. Sinolingua, 1994.

[19] Hou Fangmiao. *English for International Business Communication*. Publishing House of Electronic Industry, 2010.

[20] Zou Xiurong. *International Business Correspondence in English*. Jiangxi University Press, 2010.

[21] Su Genglin. *Practical Business English Correspondence*. Southeast University Press, 2006.

[22] Gu Qianyi. *International Business English*. South China University of Technology Press, 2006.

[23] Wang Zhaohui. *Business English Correspondence*. University of International Business and Economics Press, 2005.